CATHOLIC MORNING PRAYERS

CATHOLIC MORNING PRAYERS

Monsignor Michael J. Buckley

CHARIS

SERVANT PUBLICATIONS
ANN ARBOR, MICHIGAN

© 2000 by Michael J. Buckley

Charis Books is an imprint of Servant Publications especially designed
to serve Roman Catholics.

The author and publisher are grateful to Darton, Longman & Todd
for permission to quote prayers from *Dear Father Michael*.

Published by Servant Publications
P.O. Box 8617
Ann Arbor, Michigan 48107

00 01 02 03 04 10 9 8 7 6 5 4 3 2

Printed in the United States of America
ISBN 1-56955-187-4

Cataloging-in-Publication Data on file at the Library of Congress.

CONTENTS

Introduction

DEDICATION

To the Holy Spirit who helps us when we cannot choose words to pray properly. He "himself expresses our plea in a way that could never be put into words" (Rom 8:26).

INTRODUCTION

No two people pray in exactly the same way. Prayer is as uniquely personal to us as our fingerprints. It is an encounter within ourselves with the God whom we know and in whom we believe. It is impossible to pray to an unknown God. This is why in this book of morning prayers I have emphasized the necessity of knowing who we are and the person to whom we are praying. Praying is not knowing about God. This can be learned from a book. It is personal; that means it involves knowing God personally, who he is and what his relationship is to me and what mine is to him.

I cannot teach you how to pray, but through the pages of this book, I hope I can show you how I pray. This book includes prayers I have collected and written. They express how I feel about God, my neighbor, and myself. As I draw back the veil on how I pray, I trust the exercise will help you in your journey of self-discovery through your prayer.

I have come to know and understand myself better

over the years, and this is reflected in how I pray; prayer involves the whole of my being and not just the "holy" wishful part of it. I tell God who I am, where I am, and where I want to be, because honest prayer means being true to God and being true to myself. I am who I am in prayer—prayer that is conscious and intentional and prayer that is more subliminal— because prayer finds me out, even in my silence.

Ultimately prayer is not so much about words as it is about life. Jesus said, "In your prayers do not babble as the gentiles do, for they think that by using many words they will make themselves heard" (Mt 6:7, NJB). It is a movement of the spirit within you that expresses your longing to know the mystery of yourself and God.

Prayer is a journey of discovery that goes to the depths of your being—beyond words. And prayer in faith is something so alive and active that it transforms everything we say and do into a prayer. We pray as we live and we live as we pray. Faith and prayer are two sides of the same coin, and when we pray in faith, we will come to know at a deeper level who we are and what our purpose is in life.

The command of Jesus to love God as our Father and our neighbor as ourselves is the key that unlocks this little book of morning prayers. Prayer is a learning experience through which we grow in wisdom.

Prayer, especially in the morning, gives a focus to our lives. So it was with Jesus. Mark 1 tells of his evening ministry, healing the sick, then, "Before dawn, he got up and left the house, and went off to a lonely place and prayed" (v. 35).

Like Jesus, we all need time and space for morning prayer, through which we give direction to our lives for the rest of the day. Morning prayer is as natural and necessary for us as the air we breathe. Without it, I do not feel strong enough to fulfill my ministry of healing. We all have a favorite time in our schedule for prayer. For me it has always been the morning, when I feel the Holy Spirit is with me, nourishing me with his presence, so that I am ready for whatever the day may bring. I feel sorry for the person who is too busy to pray in the morning. That person has missed out on the one thing that would bring him or her inner peace.

My advice to you in using this book of prayers is very simple: Make it your own in such a way that you grow into it and beyond it. The prayers are only the background music that help you to compose your own melody of prayer. For example, as you remember someone who needs prayer, the Holy Spirit may put the words on your lips as you move gently into spontaneous prayer. I have found this form of prayer most helpful in my spiritual life. Often I have written down these prayers, many of which appear in this little book.

Perhaps you too might feel moved to write some prayers that you feel are Spirit-inspired. Later when you reread them, they will remind you of how the Spirit spoke to you in the morning when everything was hushed and still. If you read or say them on subsequent mornings, they will become part of your morning prayer time, in which you speak to God in your own unique way.

In my own prayer life, I focus on a different aspect of God's truth and purpose each day of the week. This pattern of mine has determined the flow of this collection of morning prayers.

Sunday focuses on **God the Father.** Especially since I founded the El Shaddai Movement for Inner Healing sixteen years ago, I have grown more aware of God as my Father in a way I would never be able to express in print because it is something precious and alive within the depths of my personality. In my relationship with people who continued to trust God under the most excruciatingly painful circumstances, I discovered what loving God as my Father meant. They loved him and taught me to do the same. In every aspect of our lives, we want to know God as our Father so that no joy or sorrow we experience excludes him.

Monday draws us in prayer to knowing **God the Son.** Jesus was perfectly human, and it is to God's glory that, in all we say and do, we become more fully human, fully alive—more Christlike. We will find new insights into God the Father by looking at the perfectly human life of Jesus, Son of the Father. I know I could never think or pray as he did, but I hope my prayer life, however lacking, in some way resembles his. The only prayer Jesus taught his followers was the Our Father. He said we were to pray like this. After nearly fifty years as a priest, I am just beginning to learn what he meant—praying the will of the Father. I feel I have never said the Our Father perfectly and I never will, because I am still damaged by the effects of sin, still trying to be the person God would have me be.

On **Tuesday** we lay ourselves open to the promptings of the **Holy Spirit.** Without him our prayers would remain just words that do not penetrate the real center of our being. The Spirit makes us alive to what is happening within us and around us in the world. He gives direction not only to prayers but to our whole life in all its aspects. We become a Spirit-filled people; this makes us one with Christ as we pray in love and gratitude to the Father. The Spirit gives a God-dimension to our prayers.

Just as Christ is one with the Father, so in the Spirit we are one with Christ. The Spirit reveals to us the meaning of the words *Our Father.* In this way we are praying in the Spirit.

Wednesday turns to prayers that help us understand **ourselves** as God sees us—his beloved children, created in his image and for his glory. Learning to know and love ourselves is an essential part of prayer. If we do not know how to love ourselves, we really do not expect our prayers to be answered, because we do not consider ourselves important in God's eyes.

Thursday prayers reach out to our relationship with **others,** whom we're called to love. Our prayer in faith does not concern itself exclusively with our belief in God, but also colors every aspect of our approach to people and the world in which we live. Our prayer life itself should never take place in a vacuum. In discovering ourselves through other people, we come to a deeper appreciation of who God is.

Friday centers on the **gift of peace** that God wants to give to each of us. Many prayers here and scattered throughout the book address fear; I hope these prayers and insights will do for you what they have done so extraordinarily for me. Prayer is the perfect antidote to fear, worry, anxiety, and all those negatives that disturb and destroy our inner peace.

And **Saturday** has always been special to me because I join my prayer along with **Mary and the communion of saints.** I sit lovingly to the Catholic tradition because of what it gives me in the

Sacraments and what it has given me through my parents, family, and friends. I have never lost them, even in death, because we are part of the communion of saints. Saturday telescopes the whole history of salvation in which the living and the dead are parts of Christ's extended family to which we belong.

You won't want to say all the prayers in any one day. This is a book that will "last" more than one week. As you make the prayers your own, they will last a lifetime. Each day read prayers as the Spirit leads you, and allow the Spirit to pray in you as you reflect deeply on life and its meaning. Soon you will put the book aside and be talking with God at a personal level that is beyond merely human writing. The Spirit will be praying in you, as you open yourself to a special gift of faith that nourishes your prayer, which in turn flows into every aspect of your life.

The theology behind the daily themes flows from the Bible and insights of holy people down through the ages. Read and meditate slowly and prayerfully on the Bible passages of each day. They are God's word for you; let it become part of your very being so that your life itself is a prayer. We are indebted in our prayer life to holy people who have gone before us and left us the distilled wisdom of their lives in prayer. Prayer is the gift of the Holy Spirit, so as we pray it is important to realize the importance of other believers whose faith flowed into their prayer life. Their faith can nourish our own.

I appreciate the prayer life of other Christians, because we each in our own way are seeking the God we want to know and pray that his Holy Spirit will guide us into a deeper understanding of who God is, who we are, and why we are here.

If this book of morning prayers helps you to grow in an awareness of yourself and your destiny as a member of the Catholic Church, then its preparation and writing have been well worthwhile.

May God richly bless your morning prayer.

Michael Buckley

Part 1

GENERAL MORNING PRAYERS

Enable Us to Walk in Light

Father, as Creator of the universe, this morning you drew back the covers of darkness, of night, to enable us to walk in the light of day without stumbling or falling. Fill our minds and hearts with the light of the love of your Son, so that we may become more aware of your abiding and loving presence in every moment of this day. Help us to become like your Son, so that we may witness to your love for everyone by what we say and do.

M.B.

Thank You for Your Goodness

God our Father, we praise and thank you for your constant goodness to us. You are the eternal Lover of life who chose us as your own beloved children before you formed us in our mother's womb. Even when we had fallen away from you by sin, you sent your only Son Jesus to be our Savior, Brother, and Friend. He was the Light of the world who dispelled the darkness of sin.

M.B.

Morning Thanks

My God, from my heart I thank you this morning for the many blessings you have given me. I thank you for having created me and for bringing me to baptism, for having placed me in your holy Catholic Church, and for having given me so many graces and mercies through the merits of Jesus Christ. I thank your Son Jesus, for having died upon the cross that I might receive pardon for my sins and obtain my eternal salvation. I thank you for all the mercies you have given me through Jesus Christ our Lord.

M.B.

Searching for God

O Lord my God,
teach my heart this day where and how to see you,
where and how to find you....

Teach me to seek you,
and when I seek you, show yourself to me;
for I cannot seek you unless you teach me,
or find you unless you show yourself to me.
Let me seek you by desiring you,
and desire you by seeking you.
Let me find you by loving you,
and love you when I find you.

Saint Anselm

Day of Gladness

Grant us, O Lord, to pass this day in gladness and peace, without stumbling and without stain; that, reaching the eventide victorious over all temptations, we may praise you, the eternal God, who are blessed, and governs all things, world without end.

Mozarabic Liturgy

You Awaken Us ...

Lord, you awaken us to delight in your praises, for you have made us for yourself, and our hearts are restless until they rest in you. Help me, Lord, to know and understand which is first—to call on you or to praise you? To know you or to call on you? For who can call on you, not knowing you?... Or is it better that we call on you that we may know you?

Saint Augustine

To Know, Love, and Serve You

Eternal God, the Light of the minds that know you, the joy of the hearts that love you, and the strength of the wills that serve you, grant us so to know you, that we may truly love you, and so to love you that we may fully serve you, whom to serve is perfect freedom, in Jesus Christ our Lord.

Saint Augustine

God Who Sees All

My God, I firmly believe that you are here and see me perfectly, and that you observe all my actions, all my thoughts, and the most secret movements of my heart. As another day dawns, you permit me, a sinner who has so often offended you, to remain in your presence, and it is your goodness and bounty that command me to come to you. Give me grace, therefore, to pray as I should, and send your Holy Spirit upon me to kindle in my heart the fire of your love.

M.B.

Daily Offering

Heavenly Father, I offer you the life and death of your Son, and with them my affections and resolutions, my thoughts, words, deeds, and sufferings this day and all my life, to honor your adorable majesty, to thank you for all your benefits, to satisfy for my sins, and to obtain the assistance of your grace, so that I may persevere to the end in doing your holy will and love and enjoy you forever in your glory.

M.B.

Do Not Leave Me to Myself

God our Father, you know how weak I am. Do not leave me to myself today but take me under your protection and give me grace to act upon my holy resolutions. Enlighten my understanding with a lively faith, raise up my will to a firm hope, and inflame it with an ardent charity. Strengthen my weakness and cure the corruption of my heart. Grant that I may overcome the enemies of my soul, and that I may make good use of your grace. And if it be that I should die today, grant me the gift of final perseverance.

M.B.

Thy Will Be Done

Lord, thy will be done in father, mother, child, in everything and everywhere—without a reserve, without a "but," an "if," or a limit.

Saint Francis de Sales

Free From Harm This Day

Now that the daylight fills the sky,
We lift our hearts to God on high,
That he, in all we do or say,
Would keep us free from harm this day.

Sixth Century, trans. by John M. Neale

Come, Light

Come, Light serene and still!
Our darkened spirits fill
    With thy clear day:
Guide of the feeble sight,

Star of grief's darkest night,
Reveal the path of right,
    Show us thy way.

Robert II of France

Teach Me Thy Love to Know

Teach me thy love to know;
That this new light, which now I see,
May both the work and workman show:
Then by a sunbeam I will climb to thee.

George Herbert

Teach Us

Teach us, good Lord, to serve you as you deserve, to give and not to count the cost, to fight and not to heed the wounds, to toil and not to seek for rest, to labor and not to ask for any reward, save that of knowing that we do your will, through Jesus Christ our Lord.

Saint Ignatius Loyola

Guide Me, Today

Heavenly Father, Protector of all who trust in you, you led your people in safety through the desert and brought them to a land of plenty. Guide me as I begin my journey today. Fill me with your Spirit of love. Preserve me from all harm and bring me safely to my destination. I ask this through Christ our Lord.

M.B.

Pilgrim Prayer

Father, you have called us this day to a pilgrimage of faith. The light of your truth summons us, and the call of faith is a constant challenge on our journey. We give thanks for the desire to seek you: We give thanks for voices from the past that offer guidance, for signposts pointing to the next stage, for companions who share the journey, for footsteps in the sand of pilgrims before us, for the conviction that, unseen but not unknown, you are with us. Father, keep us faithful to the vision and steadfast on our pilgrimage, so that the distant goal may become a reality and faith at last may lead to sight.

M.B.

Morning Blessing

May God support us all the day long, till the shades lengthen, and the evening comes, and the busy world is hushed, and the fever of life is over, and our work is done! Then in his mercy, may he give us a safe lodging, and a holy rest, and peace at the last.

John Henry Newman

O Teach My Heart

If I am right, thy grace impart
Still in the right to stay;
If I am wrong, O teach my heart
To find that better way.

Alexander Pope

Grant Us Eyes

Lord, grant us eyes to see
Within the seed a tree,
Within the glowing egg a bird,
Within the shroud a butterfly:
Till taught by such, we see
Beyond all creatures thee,
And hearken for thy tender word
And hear it, "Fear not: it is I."

Christina Rossetti

Come and Teach Us

O Wisdom, which came forth out of the mouth of the
Most High and reaches from one end to the other, mightily and sweetly ordering all things: Come and teach us the
way of prudence.

Phillips Brooks, based on Wisdom 8:1, 7

O Light of Souls

O Light of souls,
    Let us not walk in darkness.
By the Love whereby you caused the blind to see:
    Enlighten our minds with the Spirit of truth.

From Book of Litanies

Lord, Bow Down

O Lord, bow down and stay with me,
And I shall love to be with thee;
This is the end of my desire,
A heart made one with thee.

Thomas à Kempis

I Give Myself Today

Lord, in my simple heart I give myself today to be your servant ever, to listen to you and be a sacrifice of everlasting praise.

Thomas à Kempis

Let Us See Light

O thou who alone makes all contradictions clear, in your light let us see light.

Illuminate our minds with practice of humility, and confirm them with growth of faith.

Make our thoughts the lively echoes of your commandments, and take our hearts for your kingdom.

From Book of Litanies

Lord, I Ask This Day

Lord, I believe in you; increase my faith.
I trust in you; strengthen my trust.
I love you; let me love you more and more.
I am sorry for my sins; deepen my sorrow.

I worship you as my first Beginning.
I long for you as my last End.
I praise you as my constant Helper,
and call on you as my loving Protector.

Guide me by your wisdom.
Correct me with your justice,
Comfort me with your mercy.
Protect me with your power.

I offer you, Lord, my thoughts: to be fixed on you;
my words: to have you for their theme;

my actions: to reflect my love for you;
my sufferings: to be endured for your greater glory.

I want to do what you ask of me—
in the way you ask,
for as long as you ask,
because you ask it.

Lord, enlighten my understanding,
strengthen my will,
purify my heart,
and make me holy.
Help me to repent of my past sins
and to resist temptation in the future.
Help me to rise above my human weaknesses
and to grow stronger as a Christian.

Let me love you, my Lord and my God,
and see myself as I really am:
a pilgrim in this world,
a Christian called to respect and love
all whose lives I touch,
those in authority over me
or those under my authority,
my friends and my enemies.

Help me to conquer anger with gentleness,
greed with generosity,
apathy with fervor.
Help me to forget myself
and reach out to others.

Make me prudent in planning,
courageous in taking risks.

Make me patient in suffering,
unassuming in prosperity.

Keep me, Lord, attentive at prayer,
temperate in food and drink,
diligent in my work,
firm in my intentions.

Let my conscience be clear,
my conduct without fault,
my speech blameless,
my life well ordered.

Put me on my guard against my human weaknesses.
Let me cherish your love for me,
keep your law,
and come at last to your salvation.

Teach me to realize that this world is passing,
that my future is the happiness of heaven,
that life on earth is short,
and the life to come eternal.

Help me to prepare for death
with a proper fear of judgment,
but a greater trust in your goodness.
Lead me safely through death
to the endless joy of heaven.
Grant this through Christ our Lord.

Pope Clement XI

A Blessing

Lord Jesus,

Bless my memory this day that it may ever recollect you.

Bless my understanding that it may ever think of you.

Bless my will that it may never seek or desire that which may be displeasing to you.

Bless my body and all its actions.

Bless my heart with all its affections.

Bless me now and at the hour of my death.

Bless me in time and in eternity, and grant that your most sweet blessing may be to me a pledge of eternal happiness.

Bless my brethren, the faithful.

Bless my dear ones.

Bless everyone I love, and everyone to whom I owe any gratitude, and bring me and them to rest in your sacred heart forever.

M.B.

Begin the Day With God

Every morning lean thine arms awhile
Upon the windowsill of heaven
And gaze upon thy Lord.
Then, with the vision in thy heart,
Turn strong to meet thy day.

Author Unknown

Thank You for Waking Me

Lord Jesus, you are closer to me than my own breathing, as present and as life-giving as my own heart. May my every breath and heartbeat this day deepen my awareness of your presence. I thank you for waking me to the light of day. Grant that I may pass this day in gladness and peace with everyone I work with and everyone I meet, so that at day's end I shall know you have been with me, because you have been gracious enough to fill my life with your presence.

M.B.

Lord, I Offer You All That I Am

Lord Jesus, I offer you all that I am this day. I offer you:
my mind that it may be open to your understanding of the
    meaning of life,
my mouth to speak your words of peace,
my feet to follow where you would lead me,
my eyes to see the world as you do,
my sensitivity to the pain of people around me,
my faith to believe in God as my Father in the midst of suf-
    fering,
my hope to heal those you would heal through me,
my love of others to reflect your love for everyone,
my whole being that I may grow through your Spirit in
    wisdom and age before God and my fellowmen.

M.B.

Thy Will Be Done

O Lord Jesus Christ, who has created me and ordered my course and brought me hither where I am—you know what you would do with me; do so according to your will, with mercy.

King Henry VI

Open to the Holy Spirit

O God, to whom all hearts are open, hearts known, and from whom no secrets are hidden, cleanse the thoughts of our hearts by the inpouring of your Holy Spirit, that every thought and word of ours may begin from you and in you be perfectly completed, through Christ our Lord.

Adapted from The Book of Common Prayer

My Morning Song

O Lord of life, thy quickening voice awakes my morning song!
In gladsome words I would rejoice that I to thee belong.
I see thy light, I feel thy wind; the world, it is thy word;
Whatever wakes my heart and mind thy presence is, my Lord.
Therefore I choose my highest part, and turn my face to thee,
Therefore I stir my inmost heart to worship fervently.

George Macdonald

Faith and Works

The things that we pray for, good Lord, give us grace to labor for.

Saint Thomas More

Waking to My God

Oh how oft I wake and find
I have been forgetting thee!
I am never from thy mind:
Thou it is that wakest me.

George Macdonald

God Be in My Head

God be in my head,
And in my understanding;
God be in my eyes,
And in my looking;
God be in my mouth,
And in my speaking;
God be in my heart,
And in my thinking;
God be at my end,
And at my departing.

The Sarum Primer

Direct This Day

Lord, I my vows to you renew;
Disperse my sins as morning dew:
Guard my first springs of thought and will,
And with yourself my spirit fill.

Direct, control, suggest this day
All I design, or do, or say;
That all my powers, with all their might,
In your sole glory may unite.

Thomas Ken

Guide the Day

O God, creation's secret Force,
Yourself unmoved, all motion's Source,
You, from the morn till evening's ray,
Through all its changes guide the day.

Saint Ambrose of Milan, trans. by John M. Neale

Quench the Flames of Strife

O God of truth, O Lord of might,
You order time and change aright,
You send the early morning ray,
And light the glow of perfect day:
Quench now on earth the flames of strife;
From passion's heat preserve our life;
And while you keep our body whole,
Pour healing peace upon our soul.

Saint Ambrose of Milan, trans. by John M. Neale

Prayer for Today

Who can tell what a day may bring? Therefore, gracious God, cause me to live every day as if it were my last, for I know not: It may indeed be. Cause me to live now as I shall wish I had done when I come to die.

Thomas à Kempis

This Is the Day

This is the day the Lord hath made,
He calls the house his own;
Let heaven rejoice, let earth be glad,
And praise surround the throne.

Isaac Watts

Laughter and Kind Faces

The day returns and brings us the petty round of irritating concerns and duties.... Help us to perform them with laughter and kind faces. Let cheerfulness abound with industry. Give us to go blithely on our business all this day.

Bring us to our resting beds weary and content and undishonored, and grant us in the end the gift of sleep.

Robert Louis Stevenson

Morning Prayer for Family

Today we go forth separate, some of us to pleasure, some of us to worship, some upon duty. Go with us, our guide and angel; hold thou before us in our divided paths the mark of our low calling, still to be true to what small best we can attain to. Help us in that, our Maker, the dispenser of events—thou, of the vast designs, in which we blindly labor, suffer us to be so far constant to ourselves and our beloved.

Robert Louis Stevenson

Not Judas, Not I

O Jesus, watch over me always, especially today, or I shall betray you like Judas.

Saint Philip Neri

Guardian Prayer

Angel of God, my guardian dear,
To whom his love commits me here,
Ever this day be at my side
To light and rule, to guard and guide.

Traditional

Grant That None May Love You Less

Grant, O Lord, that none may love you less this day because of me; that never word or act of mine may turn one soul from you; and, ever daring, yet one other grace would I implore, that many souls this day, because of me, may love you more.

M.B.

I Sing as I Arise

I sing as I arise today!
I call on my Creator's might:
The will of God to be my guide,
The eye of God to be my sight.
The word of God to be my speech,
The hand of God to be my stay,
The shield of God to be my strength,
The path of God to be my way.
    Christ be with me, Christ before me,
    Christ behind me, Christ within me,
    Christ beneath me, Christ above me,
    Christ at my right hand, Christ at my left...
    Christ in the heart of every man who thinks of me,
    Christ in the mouth of every man who speaks to me,
    Christ in every eye that sees me,
    Christ in every ear that hears me.

Saint Patrick, "Breastplate"

Part 2

SUNDAY:

KNOWING
GOD
AS MY
FATHER

INTRODUCTION

For Christians, prayer is a personal encounter with God, our loving Father. Even though everyone is part of his family, because every human being is created in God's own image and likeness, we Christians belong to him in a unique way. He has chosen us who are in his only Son Jesus Christ—our Savior, Brother, and Friend—to be his special family. As we as Christ's brothers and sisters pray to God our Father, it is important for us to know who the heavenly Father is and learn what our attitude towards him should be. For starters, he wants to have a loving, personal relationship with us in Christ.

God is our Father in a unique way, prompting Jesus in Matthew 23:9 to say that we are to "call no one on earth your father, since you have only one Father, and he is in heaven." God is the perfect Father, shown in the way he treats his children. All human fathers, however good they may be, are but pale imitations of God's fatherly qualities. He is sensitive to our weaknesses caused by the effects of sin. This is why he sent his own Son to heal us. His love for us is shown in the humanity and love of Jesus, who was Father-oriented in all he said and did. God could not love us more than he did in Jesus, and it is in this mood of love and understanding that in the morning and throughout the day we address our prayers to him as our Father. He watches over us and gently leads us through the day.

> What father among you would hand his son a stone when he asked for bread?... If you, then, who are evil, know how to give your children what is good, how much more will the heavenly Father give the Holy Spirit to those who ask him!
>
> LUKE 11:11-13

Holy One of Three

Holy, holy, holy!
Lord God almighty!
Early in the morning
Our song shall rise to thee;
Holy, holy, holy!
Merciful and mighty!
God in three persons,
Blessed Trinity!

Holy, holy, holy!
All the saints adore thee.
Casting down their golden crowns
Around the glassy sea;
Cherubim and seraphim
Falling down before thee,
Which wert, and art,
And evermore shalt be.

Holy, holy, holy!
Though the darkness hide thee,
Though the eye of sinful man
Thy glory may not see,
Only thou art holy,
There is none beside thee,
Perfect in power,
In love, and purity.

Holy, holy, holy!
Lord God almighty!
All thy works shall praise thy name,

In earth, and sky, and sea;
Holy, holy, holy!
Merciful and mighty!
God in three persons,
Blessed Trinity!

Reginald Heber

Our Father

Our Father, who art in heaven,
hallowed be thy name;
thy kingdom come;
thy will be done on earth as it is in heaven.
Give us this day our daily bread;
and forgive us our trespasses
as we forgive those who trespass against us;
and lead us not into temptation,
but deliver us from evil.
For the kingdom, the power, and the glory
are yours, now and forever.

SCRIPTURE FOR MEDITATION

Yahweh our Lord,
how majestic is your name throughout the world!...

I look up at your heavens, shaped by your fingers,
at the moon and the stars you set firm—
what are human beings that you spare a thought for them,
or the child of Adam that you care for him?

Yet you have made him little less than a god,

you have crowned him with glory and beauty,
made him lord of the works of your hands,
put all things under his feet,

sheep and cattle, all of them,
and even the wild beasts,
birds in the sky, fish in the sea
when he makes his way across the ocean.

Yahweh our Lord,
how majestic your name throughout the world!

PSALM 8:1, 3-9, NJB

Rest in God alone, my soul!
    He is the source of my hope.
He alone is my rock, my safety,
    my stronghold, so that I stand unwavering.
In God is my safety and my glory,
    the rock of my strength.

In God is my refuge; trust in him,
    you people, at all times.
Pour out your hearts to him,
    God is a refuge for us.

PSALM 62:5-8, NJB

Better your faithful love than life itself;
my lips will praise you.
Thus I will bless you all my life,
in your name lift up my hands.

All my longings fulfilled as with fat and rich foods,
a song of joy on my lips and praise in my mouth.
On my bed when I think of you,
I muse on you in the watches of the night,
for you have always been my help;
in the shadows of your wings I rejoice;
my heart clings to you,
your right hand supports me.

PSALM 63:3-8, NJB

Lord, you have been our refuge
from age to age.

Before the mountains were born,
before the earth and the world came to birth,
from eternity to eternity you are God....

The span of our life is seventy years—
eighty for those who are strong—
but their whole extent is anxiety and trouble,
they are over in a moment and we are gone....

Each morning fill us with your faithful love,
we shall sing and be happy all our days;
let our joy be as long as the time that you afflicted us,
the years when we experienced disaster.

PSALM 90:1-2, 10, 14-15, NJB

Forgive Our Ignorance

God our Father, we find it difficult to come to you, because our knowledge of you is so imperfect. In our ignorance we have imagined you to be our enemy; we have wrongly thought that you take pleasure in punishing our sins; and we have foolishly conceived you to be a tyrant over human life.

But since Jesus came among us, he has shown that you are loving, that you are on our side against all that stunts life, and that our resentment against you was groundless.

So we come to you, asking you to forgive our past ignorance, and wanting to know more and more of you and your forgiving love, through Jesus Christ our Lord.

M.B.

God's Love as a Father

I believe that because you are my Father, you know and love me better than I know and love myself. You remind me that you are my loving Father especially at times when I seem to forget you. You say:

Does a woman forget her baby at the breast,
or fail to cherish the [child] of her womb?
Yet even if these forget
I will never forget you (Is 49:15).

M.B.

God Leads Us Kindly

All my life, because I was your child,
even without my knowing or acknowledging it,
you took me in your arms

and led me "with reins of kindness,
with leading strings of love."
You were "like someone who lifts an infant close against
  his cheek;
stooping down to give him food" (Hos 11:3-4).

M.B.

I Want to Know and Love God

My God, I pray that I may so know you and love you that
I may rejoice in you. And if I may not do so fully in this
life, let me go steadily on to the day when I come to that
fullness.

Let the knowledge of you increase in me here, and
there let it come to its fullness. Let your love grow in me
here, and there let it be fulfilled, so that here my joy may
be in a great hope, and there in full reality.

M.B.

That Your Joy May Be Full

Heavenly Father, your Son has told us that when we ask,
we will receive, so that our joy may be full. May your Holy
Spirit counsel us so that we may ask only for those things
that are truly according to your will. As we wait for your
loving response, may we give you thanksgiving and praise
that you have already answered our prayers in a way that
for the moment we may not fully understand.

M.B.

Who Are You?

Who are you then, my God? What but the Lord God? For who is Lord but the Lord? Or who is God save our God? Most highest, most good, most potent, most omnipotent; most merciful, yet most just; most hidden, yet most present; most beautiful, yet most strong; stable, yet incomprehensible; unchangeable, yet all-changing; never new, never old; all-renewing, and bringing age upon the proud though they know it not; ever working, ever at rest; still gathering, yet nothing lacking; supporting, filling, and overspreading; creating, nourishing, and maturing; seeking, yet having all things....

Oh! That I might repose on you. Oh! That you would enter into my heart and inebriate it, that I may forget my ills and embrace you, my sole Good. What are you to me? In your pity, teach me to utter it.

Saint Augustine

Help My Unbelief

Father, even though we believe in you, we still need the grace to overcome our unbelief. We hope in you and yet we worry about what may happen to us throughout this day. We love you and still seek our own will in so many ways. Accept this morning our faith, hope, and love, little though they may be, and grant that throughout this day we may grow in our belief, hope, and love of you. Through Christ our Lord.

M.B.

Let Me Never Lose Sight of You

O God, give me your grace so that the things of this earth and things more naturally pleasing to me may not be as close as you are to me. Keep my eyes, my ears, my heart from clinging to the things of this world. Break my bonds, raise my heart. Keep my whole being fixed on you. Let me never lose sight of you; and while I gaze on you, let my love of you grow more and more every day.

John Henry Newman

Bring Us to Heaven

Bring us, O Lord God,
at our last awakening into the house
and gate of heaven,
to enter into that gate and dwell in that house,
where there shall be no darkness nor dazzling,
but one equal light;
no noise nor silence,
but one equal music;
no fears nor hopes,
but one equal possession;
no ends nor beginnings,
but one equal eternity;
in the habitations of thy majesty and thy glory,
world without end.

John Donne

O Gracious and Holy Father

O Gracious and holy Father, grant us wisdom to perceive you, diligence to seek you, patience to wait for you, eyes to see you, a heart to meditate upon you, and a life to proclaim you, through the power of the Spirit of Jesus Christ our Lord.

Saint Benedict

Here and Everywhere

Father, the poet rightly says,
    "There is no place where God is not.
    Wherever I go, there God is."
Help me to realize that in my going out to meet you, you were within me all the time as my Father loving me and shielding me with your presence even though in my foolishness I thought you had left me to walk alone.

M.B.

Help Me Always to Thank You

O Father, whose mercy is boundless and whose gifts are without end, help me always to thank you for everything that your loving power has bestowed on me. Make me realize that my desire to thank you is itself your gift, and that my thankfulness is never-ending because your loving is never-failing.

M.B.

Eyes of Faith

Father, faith is a precious gift that gives me new insights into the wonderful things in our world hidden behind the facade of glitz and glamour. Because we are human, there are times when we obscure even great spiritual events. Today, I thank you, Father, that your Son came to our world into a humble loving home; that he grew to manhood as a simple carpenter in the village shop of Nazareth; that he shared our life, with all its sorrows and joy. May I borrow his eyes this day and look on my world with his vision of peace; may I see the glory of your beauty, which is hidden except to those who look with eyes of faith.

M.B.

A Family Prayer

Father, thank you for having created us and given us to each other in the human family. Thank you for being with us in all our joys and sorrows, for your comfort in our sadness, your companionship in our loneliness. Thank you for family, for friends, and for your loving presence among us. Bring peace to all those who suffer discord in their families, and grant that they be reconciled to each other so that your peace may descend on them and remain always with them. Grant that they will grow as a loving family which shares a life together in love and harmony.

M.B.

In God—My All

God, of your goodness, give me yourself for you are sufficient for me. If I were to ask anything less, I should always be in want, for in you alone do I have all.

Julian of Norwich

Grateful for Your Creation

Father, loving Creator of all life, help us to be grateful for the companionship of animals. May we treat them with compassion, as gifts from you entrusted to our care, and never subject them to cruelty or neglect. May the charge you give us over them be a partnership of mutual service, so that through them we may come to a greater appreciation of your glory in creation. May we respond to their loyalty to us by showing them that, in a special way under your gentle guidance, they are for our happiness and fulfillment in your loving creation.

M.B.

Father, Tender as a Mother

Father, you treat us as tenderly as an eagle who supports her young on her wings as they learn to fly. Be with us today and every day as we witness to your Son Jesus Christ, who gave his life as a testimony of his love for you and for us. May we never be afraid to proclaim your never-failing love, so that through sharing our faith with others, they may learn to believe that you are tender and loving to them as only a loving parent could be.

M.B.

Father Who Heals

God our Father, slow to anger and swift to compassion, make me realize that you never punish me for my sins, but forgive me more readily than I am prepared to forgive myself. Your Son Jesus told us to forgive our neighbor only as we forgive ourselves, so that if I do not forgive myself, I am unable to forgive my neighbor. You are not a severe judge who watches over our every action and writes down everything we do wrong. You want to be known for what you are, a loving, forgiving Father who heals and forgives us because we are your children.

M.B.

Sunday Prayer

Heavenly Father, I thank you that on this special day of the week we commemorate the resurrection of Jesus your only Son. He has given our lives new hope and purpose by rising from the dead. We thank you for Holy Mass, through which we offer to you, Father, the supreme sacrifice of your Son for our salvation.

We are blessed by the good news of the gospel, the singing of the hymns in which we raise our voices to you in praise and adoration. We thank you for our brothers and sisters who share in our faith and love for you.

We cannot find words to praise you for the gift of your Son in Holy Communion by which we are strengthened for the rest of this day, week, and life.

We pray for those who have gone before us whose prayers and efforts helped to raise this church for your honor and glory. May we go forth from this place conscious of your love, and may we never stray far from the memory of your presence on this Sunday which you have blessed through the resurrection of Jesus your Son.

M.B.

Sunday Set Aside

O God our Father, we thank you that you have taught us to set aside one day in the week where we can relax freely from the burdens that each day brings. Help us to be mindful of the presence of your Son Jesus Christ, whose resurrection we celebrate. Send your Holy Spirit to be with us this morning in our church service in which we give you thanks for the treasure of our Christian faith.

May we spend more time with you throughout this day and refresh our inner spirit with memories of your loving care for us. Strengthen us so that we may never forget you in the days of the week that lie ahead. Bless those with whom we share this morning's worship and make us aware not only of their friendship, but also of the trials they may be going through as we pray with and for them so that they too may give you praise and thanksgiving for your loving, healing presence in their lives.

M.B.

Bless Those Not at Church

Heavenly Father we pray for all those who cannot come to church today:

those who are ill;

those who will spend this day looking after a loved one who is in need of special care;

those who are too old and infirm to venture outside their homes;

those who must work, even on Sunday;

those who feel that religion has no part in their lives;

those whose home-life is so shattered and unhappy that

they cannot face the ordeal of praying and singing in
church;

those who are dying and for whom this is their last Sunday;

the babies who are born today and who will worship in this
church long after we have passed on;

those who are sad and disillusioned with life so that
Sunday is no different from any other dreary and
depressing day;

those who are young and feel religion is out-of-date;

those who feel unworthy and unforgiven;

those who through our prayers, compassion, and friendli-
ness will venture into church next Sunday seeking their
home like the Prodigal Son.

For these and many others whom we cannot remember
but whom you love, we pray that they know that you are
with them wherever they are, if only they allow your Holy
Spirit to speak to their minds and hearts.

M.B.

As Children We Look to You

Heavenly Father, give us your grace to live this day to the
full. May we fill it with all the wonder and joy we knew as
children. Let us never lose sight of the fact that no matter
what may happen this day, you are our Father who loves
us in your special way and wants our health, healing, and
happiness, through Christ our Lord.

M.B.

Know, Love, Serve

Father, we ask the grace through every moment of this day:

to know you more clearly as our first beginning and last end;

to love you as being everything our heart could desire and need;

to serve you in everyone we meet so that they may see your presence in all we say and do.

M.B.

Live in Us Throughout the Day

God my loving Father, you sent your Son Jesus to earth; he took his flesh from the Virgin Mary; may you live in us, unworthy as we are, so that your Son may live in us from sunrise to sunset of this day as we witness in the Spirit to your fatherly love for everyone.

M.B.

No God Like You

O God our loving Father,

teach us this day how to know, love, and serve you, because there is no God like you who could know, love, and serve us as you have done. When we were wounded by sin, you sent your Son Jesus to heal us. Bless my soul, mind, and body this day, so that all I say and do may bring honor to your Son, whose witnesses we are, and glory to you our loving Father, who wants what is best for us. We make this prayer in the power of the Spirit, who lives in us as the gift of you and your Son Jesus.

M.B.

Brighten Our World
Father in heaven, you have given us a mind to know you, a desire to serve you, and a heart to love you. Be with us today in all that we say and do so that your light may shine through to brighten the darkness of our world and help fill the emptiness in people's lives.

M.B.

May I Find You Near Me
Father, turn my mind and thoughts toward you this day, so that in all the distractions the day may bring, I find you near me and within me, bringing me peace and happiness.

M.B.

A Song of Creation
Bless the Lord, all the Lord's creation:
praise and glorify him for ever!
Bless the Lord, angels of the Lord,
praise and glorify him for ever!
Bless the Lord, heavens,
praise and glorify him for ever!...
Bless the Lord, sun and moon,
praise and glorify him for ever!...

Bless the Lord, all rain and dew,
praise and glorify him for ever!
Bless the Lord, every wind,
praise and glorify him for ever!
Bless the Lord, fire and heat,
praise and glorify him for ever!
Bless the Lord, cold and warmth,

praise and glorify him for ever!
Bless the Lord, dew and snow-storm,
praise and glorify him for ever!...
Bless the Lord, light and darkness,
praise and glorify him for ever!
Bless the Lord, lightning and cloud,
praise and glorify him for ever!

Let the earth bless the Lord:
praise and glorify him for ever!
Bless the Lord, mountains and hills,
praise and glorify him for ever!
Bless the Lord, every plant that grows,
praise and glorify him for ever!
Bless the Lord, springs of water,
praise and glorify him for ever!
Bless the Lord, seas and rivers,
praise and glorify him for ever!
Bless the Lord, whales,
    and everything that moves in the waters,
praise and glorify him for ever!
Bless the Lord, every kind of bird,
praise and glorify him for ever!
Bless the Lord, all animals wild and tame,
praise and glorify him for ever!

Bless the Lord, all the human race:
praise and glorify him for ever!...
Bless the Lord, his servants,
praise and glorify him for ever!

Bless the Lord, spirits and souls of the upright,
praise and glorify him for ever!
Bless the Lord, faithful, humble-hearted people,
praise and glorify him for ever!

From DANIEL 3:57-87, NJB

Part 3

MONDAY:

JESUS IS LORD AND SAVIOR

INTRODUCTION

Jesus Christ, the second Person of the blessed Trinity, is our Healer, Leader, Brother, Friend, and Savior. He is all these and much more.

He humbled himself to come among us as a baby, and grown to manhood he allowed himself to be crucified even though he was God's only Son. He did this to show his love for us and his Father.

We make all our prayers in the name and for the sake of Jesus Christ, who is truly God and truly man. He is the one mediator between God and us (1 Tm 2:5). He is the channel through which all our prayers flow.

As God's Son, he is Lord, but as man he became the Servant of all when he emptied himself of his divine glory during his time on earth. Jesus loved his human condition from his birth to his death. After his resurrection, he resumed his lordship and the exercise of his divine power. We could have no more powerful mediator than he as he takes all our prayers to the Father and gives them a divine dimension. The Servant who is our Savior is also now our Lord. One day we hope to share in his divine kingdom as once he came among us as a Servant to share our human condition.

Morning Praise

When morning gilds the skies,
My heart awaking cries,
May Jesus Christ be praised:
Alike at work and prayer
To Jesus I repair;
May Jesus Christ be praised!

Be this, while life is mine,
My canticle divine,
May Jesus Christ be praised:
Be this the eternal song,
Through all the ages long,
May Jesus Christ be praised!

German Hymn, trans. by Edward Caswall

Hosanna Hymn to Jesus

The company of angels is praising you on high;
And we with all creation in chorus make reply.

Theodulph of Orleans

SCRIPTURE AND QUOTES FOR MEDITATION

I am the Way; I am Truth and Life.
No one can come to the Father except through me.
If you know me, you will know my Father too.
From this moment you know him and have seen him.

JOHN 14:6-7, NJB

For this is how God loved the world:
he gave his only Son,
so that everyone who believes in him may not perish
but may have eternal life.

JOHN 3:16, NJB

The Word became flesh, he lived among us, and we saw his glory, the glory that he has from the Father as only Son of the Father, full of grace and truth.

JOHN 1:14, NJB

There is only one God, and there is only one mediator between God and humanity, himself a human being, Christ Jesus.

1 TIMOTHY 2:5, NJB

He is the sacrifice that takes our sins away,
and not only ours,
but the whole world's.

1 JOHN 2:2

He had not done anything wrong, and there had been no perjury in his mouth. He was insulted and did not retaliate with insults; when he was tortured he made no threats but he put his trust in the righteous judge. He was bearing our faults in his own body on the cross, so that we might die to our faults and live for holiness; through his wounds you have been healed.

1 PETER 2:22-24

I tell you most solemnly,
I am the gate of the sheepfold....
Anyone who enters through me will be safe:
he will go freely in and out
and be sure of finding pasture....
I am the good shepherd;
I know my own
and my own know me,
just as the Father knows me
and I know the Father;
and I lay down my life for my sheep.

JOHN 10:7, 9, 14-15

I am the resurrection, and the life.
If anyone believes in me, even though he dies he will live,
and whoever lives and believes in me
will never die.

JOHN 11:25-26

Since in Jesus, the Son of God, we have the supreme high priest who has gone through to the highest heaven, we must never let go of the faith we have professed. For it is not as if we had a high priest who was incapable of feeling our weaknesses with us; but we have one who has been tempted in every way that we are, though he is without sin. Let us be confident, then, in approaching the throne of grace that we shall have mercy from him and find grace when we are in need of help.

HEBREWS 4:14-16

Although he was Son, he learned to obey through suffering; but having been made perfect, he became for all who obey him the source of eternal salvation.

HEBREWS 5:8-9

A man can have no greater love
than to lay down his life for his friends.
You are my friends,
if you do what I command you.
I shall not call you servants any more,
because a servant does not know
his master's business;
I call you friends,
because I have made known to you
everything I have learned from my Father.

JOHN 15:13-15

His state was divine,
yet he did not cling
to his equality with God
but emptied himself
to assume the condition of a slave,
and became as men are;
and being as all men are,
he was humbler yet,
even to accepting death,
death on a cross.
But God raised him high
and gave him the name
which is above all other names
so that all beings

in the heavens, on earth and in the underworld,
should bend the knee at the name of Jesus
and that every tongue should acclaim
Jesus Christ as Lord,
to the glory of God the Father.

PHILIPPIANS 2:6-11

Ours were the sufferings he bore,
ours the sorrows he carried....
If he offers his life in atonement,
he shall see his heirs, he shall have a long life
and through him what Yahweh wishes will be done.

ISAIAH 53:4, 10

Letter From Jesus

Dear Friend,

How are you? I just had to send a note to tell you how much I care about you.

I saw you yesterday as you were talking with your friends. I waited all day hoping you would want to talk with me too. I gave you a sunset to close your day and a cool breeze to rest you—and I waited. You never came. It hurt me—but I still love you because I am your friend.

I saw you sleeping last night and longed to touch your brow so I spilled moonlight on your face. Again I waited, wanting to rush down so we could talk. I have so many gifts for you! You awoke and rushed off to work. My tears were in the rain.

If you would only listen to me! I love you! I try to tell you in blue skies and in the quiet green grass. I whisper it in leaves on the trees and breathe it in colors of flowers, shout it to you in mountain streams, give the birds love songs to sing. I clothe you with warm sunshine and perfume and air with nature's scents. My love for you is deeper than the ocean, and bigger than the biggest need in your heart!

Ask me! Talk with me! Please don't forget me. I have so much to share with you!

I won't hassle you any further. It is your decision. I have chosen you and still I wait—because I love you.

Your friend,
JESUS
Author Unknown

Children of the Kingdom

Lord Jesus, you saw trust and simplicity in children's eyes, and you told us that unless we become like them we would not enter your Father's kingdom. During your life on earth, you showed your love for children in such a gentle way that they followed you wherever you went and crowded around you. This morning keep us close to you, gentle Son of God, that we may once again, like children, rediscover the wonder of your message of love and peace for everyone that captivated us when we were young. May we be simple and trusting, so that we never lose the beauty and innocence of our youth until at last we come before our Father as children of his kingdom.

M.B.

Love of Animals as Companions

Lord Jesus, in your humility, as a lover of animals, you chose a donkey to carry you into your beloved Jerusalem; may we look upon animals as our companions and as your gift to us as together, man and beast, we journey through life and share in the beauty of your creation.

M.B.

Seeing Beyond Suffering

Lord Jesus, I have often been disturbed by suffering over which I had no control. It laid me so low and diminished me, so that I could not even think of praying. At those times I needed to remember how you suffered all through your public life, until in the end you hung rejected and abandoned on the cross. In your agony you still called God your Father, and you committed your pain, suffering, and whole life into his hands. In your attitude to suffering I find courage and hope to persevere in mine, believing that the darkness of your Calvary on Friday was lit up by the glory of your resurrection. May I look beyond the pain of my suffering to the joy of eternal life when everything in my life will find its meaning and purpose, because all my pain is taken up in the light and peace of your resurrection.

M.B.

Day by Day

Thank you, Lord Jesus Christ, for all the benefits you have won for us, for all the pain and insults you have borne for us. O most merciful Redeemer, Friend, and Brother, may we know you more clearly, love you more dearly, and follow you more nearly day by day.

Saint Richard of Chichester

Write Your Name

Write your name, Lord Jesus, upon my heart, there to remain so indelibly engraved that no prosperity, no adversity shall ever remove me from your love. Be to me a strong tower of defense, a comforter in tribulation, a deliverer in distress, an ever-present help in trouble, and a guide to heaven through the many temptations and dangers of life.

Thomas à Kempis

Newton's Prayer

O Jesus! Shepherd, Guardian, Friend,
O Prophet, Priest, and King,
My Lord, my life, my Way, my End,
Accept the praise I bring.

John Newton

Come, My Way, My Truth, My Life

Come, my Way, my Truth, my Life;
Such a way as gives us breath;
Such a truth as ends all strife;
Such a life as killeth death....

Come, my Joy, my Love, my Heart:
Such a joy as none can move;
Such a love as none can part;
Such a heart as joys in love.

George Herbert

The Same Forever and Today

We know the way: thank God who hath shown us the way!
Jesus Christ our Way to beautiful Paradise,
Jesus Christ the same forever, the same today.

Christina Rossetti

Holy Jesus, Every Day

Holy Jesus, every day
Keep us in the narrow way;
And when earthly things are past,
Bring our ransomed souls at last
Where they need no star to guide,
Where no clouds thy glory hide.

William Dix

Keep Us Close

Lord Jesus Christ, ... do not allow us to stray from you
who are the Way, to distrust you who are the Truth, or to
rest on any other than you who are the Life. Teach us what
to believe, what to do, and where to take our rest.

Desiderius Erasmus

Adore the Redeemer

We adore you, Lord Jesus Christ, in all the churches of the
world, and we bless you, for by means of your holy cross,
you have redeemed the world.

Saint Francis of Assisi

Lord, Think on Me

Lord Jesus, think on me,
And purge away my sin;
From harmful passions set me free,
And make me pure within.

Synesius of Cyrene, trans. by Allen Chatfield

In Trial

In the hour of trial, Jesus, plead for me.

James Montgomery

Come This Day

Lord Jesus Christ, you came to earth to heal a broken-hearted and wounded world. You had compassion on those who called on you for help and healing. You touched the sick and guilt-laden, and they walked away in health and freedom of spirit. Come this day to all who call on your holy name and visit them with your saving power, so that they too may be released in mind and body to praise and thank you for your love and compassion.

M.B.

May We Welcome You in the Stranger

Lord Jesus, when you lived in our world, you fed the hungry in the desert and told the apostles that it was their duty to look after the hungry. When we thank you for our food and the shelter of our home, remind us—in our minds and hearts—to make hospitality our special care, so that the stranger will always find a welcome at our door and a place at our table, because in welcoming him we will be welcoming you.

M.B.

Gentle Shepherd

Lord Jesus Christ, no matter what dangers we are placed in remind us always to call upon your name, because you are the Shepherd who will lead us into fresh pastures where peace will reign and the terror of darkness will be no more.

M.B.

Good Samaritan Prayer

Lord Jesus, who was wounded for our sins that we might be healed and live the new life of grace, we thank you for all those who throughout our lives have come unbidden to our aid. They have been the Good Samaritans who have made your gospel come alive for us. Grant that we too may always consider it a privilege to come to the assistance of those in trouble, even strangers, knowing that whenever we assist them we are really tending the wounded Christ in them.

M.B.

Be Present in Our Churches

Jesus Christ, when you were on earth, people saw, heard, and touched you as you walked and lived among them. Today, you live in your Church under sacramental signs. This means we need faith to believe that you are still with us. It is impossible for us to convey your presence unless and until we experience you personally. It is only when you showed yourself to me in people, Lord, that I became aware of your presence. I found you in:

the sick and the lonely;

the young and the old, who were searching for a meaning to life;

the rich and the poor, who felt that there was something
   else more important than security and wealth;
the healthy and the dying, who believed that you were the
   Resurrection and the Life.
In all these people I found you.

Now I know that a church is only a building unless you
live in the lives of those who come to worship. Acts of worship in our churches are only rituals without meaning
unless those who perform them are filled with, and yearn
for, your presence.

Be present, Lord, in our churches and places of worship, especially in the minds and hearts of the young, so
that they see beyond external actions and reach out in love
to those around them in whom they see your abiding presence.

M.B.

Friend of the Poor

Lord Jesus, Friend of the poor, you gave us the perfect
example of what our attitude to rank and power should be.
You said if we wanted to be fulfilled, we should seek the
kingdom of your Father first, and everything else would
fall into place. Power, as the world understands it, was
something you avoided; you told your followers that if
they were to be like you, they were not to court secular
power, because your kingdom was not of this world.
Guide my footsteps so that I never stray from the true
path; you are my only way to the Father whom I wish to
serve in all that I say and do.

M.B.

Servant of All

Lord Jesus Christ, we praise you that you came to earth as the Servant of all. Having compassion on the people, you took them where you found them; as a kindly Shepherd, you showed them the way to pastures new. Teach us always to see ourselves as part of a loving, caring, sharing community in which we learn from each other your gentle service and care of others.

M.B.

Encourage What Is Good in People

Jesus, when you were on earth, you enjoyed the company of publicans and sinners, because you knew the good that was within people. Teach us to feel and live out your love and peace, that we may never prejudge others harshly or speak a cruel word, but always encourage what is good in others, so that our community may be blessed with harmony, goodwill, and peace.

M.B.

Lighten Me, Good Jesus

Lighten me, good Jesus, with the bright light within,
And from my heart's cell drive away all shadows.
Bridle my many wandering thoughts;
Fight bravely for me, conquer the wild beasts—
Enticing lusts, I mean—
That in your strength there may be peace,
And that your praise may evermore resound
Within your holy temple—
A conscience that is pure.

Thomas à Kempis

From Fears Release Us

Come, thou long-expected Jesus,
Born to set thy people free;
From our fears and sins release us,
Let us find our rest in thee.

Israel's strength and consolation,
Hope of all the earth thou art:
Dear desire of every nation,
Joy of every longing heart.

Charles Wesley

I Am Sometimes Afraid

I am sometimes afraid, because there seems to be no direction in my life, and I am not sure where I am going. At these times, when I seem lost and walking in the world of shadows, I turn to you, Lord Christ—the Good Shepherd who gave your life for your sheep—knowing that you will lead me along the right path and keep me safe from harm. May I always hear your voice amid life's storms, and may it be like music to my ears bringing me peace.

M.B.

Teach Me to Contemplate You

O most tender and gentle Lord Jesus, when will my heart have a portion of your perfections? When will my hard and stony heart, my proud heart, my unbelieving, my impure heart, my narrow selfish heart, be melted and conformed to yours? O teach me so to contemplate you that I may become like you, and to love you sincerely and simply as you have loved me.

John Henry Newman

Seeing Beyond Death

Lord Jesus, I praise and thank you more than words could express that in your humility and love for us you came among us as an innocent baby. You suffered and died to restore and heal us. When you rose from the dead, you destroyed our fear of death. It can no longer claim absolute victory over us, because now we have the vision and hope that your resurrection brings.

Lift us, strong Son of God, so that from your cross, and borrowing your eyes, we may see beyond death to a new horizon of hope and life without end.

M.B.

Bereavement and Hope

Lord Jesus, Lover of life, who died and rose again so that we might be comforted at the death of a loved one, be with all those who today are bereaved and whose lives are drastically changed by the death of a loved one. Help them to see beyond the grave to the brightness of new life, and grant that one day they will be reunited with their loved one in heaven, where there will be no more mourning or weeping but only the happiness of everlasting life together.

M.B.

Fill Our Hearts With Love

Lord Jesus, you came among us and by your example showed that love is the greatest commandment; without it all religious observances are meaningless. Fill our hearts with love for God our Father, and through love may we live at peace with our neighbor and within ourselves.

M.B.

Jesus, Our Great Encourager

Lord Jesus, almighty Son of God, you too needed encouragement during your ministry on earth. We praise you that in your risen life you are our great Encourager; even when we walk in the valley of darkness, you are there as the Good Shepherd with your crook and staff to give us comfort. Help us today in word and deed to be a source of encouragement to everyone we meet.

M.B.

We Turn Again

Jesus, thou Joy of loving hearts,
Thou Fount of life, thou Light of men,
From the best bliss that earth imparts
We turn unfilled to thee again.

We taste thee, O thou living Bread,
And long to feast upon thee still;
We drink of thee, the Fountain-head,
And thirst our souls from thee to fill.

Eleventh-Century Latin Hymn, trans. by Ray Palmer

Jesus, the Very Thought of Thee

Jesus, the very thought of thee
With sweetness fills my breast;
But sweeter far thy face to see,
And in thy presence rest.

No voice can sing, no heart can frame,
Nor can the memory find
A sweeter sound than thy blest name,
O Savior of mankind.

O Hope of every contrite heart,
O Joy of all the meek,
To those who fall, how kind thou art,
How good to those who seek!

But what to those who find? Ah, this
Nor tongue nor pen can show:
The love of Jesus, what it is,
None but his lovers know.

Jesus, our only joy be thou,
As thou our prize will be;
Jesus, be thou our glory now,
And through eternity.

Saint Bernard of Clairvaux,
trans. by Edward Caswall

Part 4

TUESDAY:

THE
HOLY SPIRIT
OF GOD

INTRODUCTION

The Holy Spirit lives in each one of us and teaches us how to pray. The Spirit is our soul mate and inspiration. He encourages us to look on God as our Father and Jesus as our Friend and Lord of our lives. With the Holy Spirit we are never alone when we pray. He lifts us up in every situation in which we find ourselves and fills us with love, trust, and joy in our Christian lives.

Prayer without the Holy Spirit would be empty words. He is the gift to us of both the Father and of Jesus Christ, his only Son which enables us to live a Christian life. He gives our lives a meaning greater than any merely human dimension. He prays in us as Christ would pray in our world and situation. Through him the risen Christ lives in us in a unique way. He is the Spirit of love which links us into the life of the Blessed Trinity.

Come Down, O Love

Come down, O Love divine,
Seek thou this soul of mine,
And visit it
With thine own ardor glowing;
O Comforter, draw near,
Within my heart appear,
And kindle it,
Thy holy flame bestowing.

O let it freely burn,
Till earthly passions turn
To dust and ashes
In its heat consuming;
And let thy glorious Light
Shine ever on my sight,
And clothe me round,
The while my path illuming.

Let holy charity
Mine outward vesture be,
And lowliness become
Mine inner clothing;
True lowliness of heart,
Which takes the humbler part,
And o'er its own
Shortcomings weeps with loathing.

Bianco da Siena, trans. by Richard Littledale

SCRIPTURE FOR MEDITATION

I shall pour clean water over you and you will be cleansed;
I shall cleanse you of all your filth and of all your foul idols.
I shall give you a new heart, and put a new spirit in you; I
shall remove the heart of stone from your bodies and give
you a heart of flesh instead. I shall put my spirit in you, and
make you keep my laws, and respect and practise my
judgements. You will live in the country which I gave your
ancestors. You will be my people and I shall be your God.

EZEKIEL 36:25-28, NJB

I shall ask the Father,
and he will give you another Advocate
to be with you for ever,
that Spirit of truth
whom the world can never receive
since it neither sees nor knows him;
but you know him,
because he is with you, he is in you.
I will not leave you orphans.

JOHN 14:16-18

When the Spirit of truth comes
he will lead you to the complete truth,
since he will not be speaking as from himself
but will say only what he has learned;
and he will tell you of the things to come.
He will glorify me,
since all he tells you
will be taken from what is mine.

JOHN 16:13-14

When Pentecost day came round, [the apostles] had all met in one room, when suddenly they heard what sounded like a powerful wind from heaven, the noise of which filled the entire house in which they were sitting; and something appeared to them that seemed like tongues of fire; these separated and came to rest on the head of each of them. They were all filled with the Holy Spirit, and began to speak foreign languages as the Spirit gave them the gift of speech.

ACTS 2:1-4

All who are guided by the Spirit of God are sons of God; for what you received was not the spirit of slavery to bring you back into fear; you received the spirit of adoption, enabling us to cry out, "*Abba,* Father!" The Spirit himself joins with our spirit to bear witness that we are children of God. And if we are children, then we are heirs, heirs of God and joint-heirs with Christ, provided that we share his suffering, so as to share his glory.

ROMANS 8:14-17, NJB

No one can say, "Jesus is Lord," unless he is under the influence of the Holy Spirit.

1 CORINTHIANS 12:3

The Spirit too comes to help us in our weakness. For when we cannot choose words in order to pray properly, the Spirit himself expresses our plea in a way that could never be put into words, and God who knows everything in our hearts knows perfectly well what he means, and that the pleas of the saints expressed by the Spirit are according to the mind of God.

ROMANS 8:26-27

There is a variety of gifts but always the same Spirit; there are all sorts of service to be done, but always to the same Lord; working in all sorts of different ways in different people, it is the same God who is working in all of them. The particular way in which the Spirit is given to each person is for a good purpose....

Now you together are Christ's body; but each of you is a different part of it.

1 CORINTHIANS 12:4-7, 27

The Finger of God

O Holy Spirit, adorable and all-powerful, the holy church calls you the Finger of God, because you proceed from the Father and the Son, as the finger from the body and the arm. You are God, like the Father and the Son, infinite, eternal, and immense. Ah! Triumph over wickedness and by the merits of Jesus Christ and his divine mother, communicate to us your gifts.

Mary of Agreda

Let Your Mercy Be Upon Us

Let your mercy, O Lord, be upon us, and the brightness of your Spirit illumine our inward souls, that the Spirit may kindle our cold hearts and light up our dark minds.

From Bright's Ancient Collects

Make This House Your Home

Spirit divine, attend our prayers,
And make this house your home.
Descend with all your gracious powers,
O come, great Spirit, come!

Andrew Reed

Descend Upon My Heart

Spirit of God, descend upon my heart....
I ask no dream, no prophet ecstasies,
No sudden rending of the veil of clay,
No angel visitant, no opening skies;
But take the dimness of my soul away.

George Croly

Holy Spirit, Faithful Guide

Holy Spirit, faithful Guide,
Ever near the Christian's side;
Gently lead us by the hand,
Pilgrims in a desert land.

Marcus Wells

Cheer My Heart

Holy Ghost, with joy divine,
Cheer this saddened heart of mine;
Bid my many woes depart,
Heal my wounded, bleeding heart.

Andrew Reed

Spirit, Dwell With Me

Gracious Spirit, dwell with me;
I myself would gracious be.
Truthful Spirit, dwell with me;
I myself would truthful be.
Holy Spirit, dwell with me;
I myself would holy be.

Thomas Lynch

Be With Us Today

Lord God, the Holy Ghost!
In this accepted hour,
As on the day of Pentecost,
Descend in all your power.

James Montgomery

To the Spirit of Light and Love

May the Holy Spirit,
the Spirit of Pentecost,
help you to clarify what is ambiguous,
to give warmth to what is indifferent,
to enlighten what is obscure,
to be before the world
true and generous witnesses of Christ's love,
for no one can live without love.

Pope John Paul II

To the Holy Spirit

As the wind is your symbol
 so forward our goings.
As the dove
 so launch us heavenwards.
As water
 so purify our spirits.
As a cloud
 so abate our temptations.
As dew
 so revive our languor.
As fire
 so purge out our dross.

Christina Rossetti

O Holy Spirit

Let me so pass through the misty desert of this world by your light going before me, that I may neither be defiled with Satan's wiles nor entangled with any errors not conforming with your truth.

Desiderius Erasmus

Your Will as Ours

Heavenly Father, grant that by the guidance of the Holy Spirit we may discern your holy will for us this day, and by the grace of the same Spirit we may also do it, gladly and with our whole hearts, for the glory of your Son Jesus Christ our Lord.

M.B.

That We May Live With Christ

Holy Spirit, make our lives new by your divine power, that we may live by the light of the resurrection and work in a manner inspired by you. May Christ, our Brother, be with us today and every day, now and forever.

M.B.

An American Indian's Prayer to God

O Great Spirit,
whose voice I hear in the winds,
and whose breath gives life to the world,
hear me.

I come to you as one of your many children.
I am small and weak.
I need your strength and your wisdom.

May I walk in beauty.
Make my eyes ever behold the red and purple sunset.
Make my hands respect the things you have made,
and my ears sharp to hear your voice.

Make me wise so that I may know
the things you have taught your children,
the lessons you have hidden in every leaf and rock.

Make me strong
so that I may not be superior to other people,
but able to fight my greatest enemy,
which is myself.

Make me ever ready to come to you with straight eyes
so that, when life fades as the fading sunset,
my spirit may come to you without shame.

Holy Spirit of Faith

Holy Spirit, we praise and thank you that you help us to
live our Christian faith in hope and joy.

You are the Inspirer of our prayers to the Father. We ask
you this morning to bless all Christians of all denominations who pray, work, and strive for unity and continue
their work of bridge building. May we never do separately
those things that in conscience we can do together. We are
all enriched by one another's gifts and ministries, of which
you are the source. Through your vibrant inspiration you
transform our set attitudes of religion into a living faith
whose witness the world needs if it is to believe in the
power and resurrection of Jesus Christ our Lord.

M.B.

The Spirit in the Bible

Holy Spirit, you guide us as we read the Bible, with its
words and stories that help us to find the strength to face
up to every situation we encounter today. Life is never
easy. There are times when, relying on our own power, we
will fail ourselves and our Christian faith. Put in our minds
and hearts through our reading of the Bible the healing we
need, which will soothe our pain and make us more open
and aware of your abiding and unchanging love for us.

M.B.

Spirit of Hope

Holy Spirit, teach us today to look on the bright side of everything, so that for us even the darkest cloud has a silver lining. Just as this day begins with light, so inspire us to turn our faces toward your radiance, so that we may reflect your light and hope to everyone we meet today—the light and hope that will lift people up and give them hope that though things may be dark right now, the clouds will lift and give way to the brightness of a new day and more hopeful life for them.

M.B.

Teach Me to Live a Resurrection Life

Holy Spirit, we come alive when we hear your gospel preached vibrantly. Your message is of life not death. You teach us how to live here and now. Nothing is outside the scope of your message. Teach us to live so that every aspect of our lives is shot through with the brilliance of Christ's resurrection. May we never withdraw from the world except to find you in prayer. Then, refreshed by you, may we go back to the bustle of the world reflecting your love and care for the people we encounter.

M.B.

Spirit of Love and Forgiveness

Holy Spirit of love and forgiveness, you know us through and through and fill us with hope. You teach us that because God is our Father, there is no such thing as an unforgivable sin as we try to be sorry for what we have done. I thank you that many times you have taken my guilt of the past away when I felt that God had deserted me because of my sinfulness. You lifted me up so that I could begin my life anew.

Today I pray that, just as you have been with me, you will also be with all those who feel weighed down by their past misdeeds and cannot find any true lasting peace; those whose sins are ever before them so that the past destroys the quality of their present life. Only you, Holy Spirit, can give them hope and heal their memories. In learning from the past and your goodness to us, may we all give you thanks for your love and mercy, as we live day by day in peace, free from fear and guilt.

M.B.

Bless My Worship

Spirit of the Living God, I praise you that each day you renew in me the message of Jesus Christ, making it my life's great challenge. You give inspiration to the acts of worship in your church, so that they and your living presence nourish me. Without you within me, I could never truly worship in word or action. I would never come to realize what prayer really means unless you pray in me and give my life meaning in all that I say and do. Be with all believers gathered together for worship. Spirit of Christ, bring them alive so that they thrill to the message of Jesus our Lord and Master.

M.B.

Thanksgiving for Faith

Holy Spirit, I give you thanks this morning that you have blessed me with the gift of faith. It is a precious gift that I want to pass along to others, especially those I love, so we would draw closer to each other as we share a bond in you. Jesus wants us to spread his good news of love, hope, and peace to a world that has not yet learned to believe in him. Give me, Holy Spirit, a deepening awareness of my faith, and a growing sensitivity to the needs of others, so that through my daily actions, demeanor, and words, I may be privileged to prepare them to receive the gift of Christian faith. Be with husbands and wives today—those whose partners do not share their faith. Help them to witness to the faith that is in them, and hear their prayers, that their loved ones be drawn to you.

M.B.

Prayer for Unity

We thank you, Holy Spirit, for the faith of all people everywhere who see a power beyond themselves as the source of their being and the preservation of their life and happiness. I praise you for all Christians, whatever their religious affiliation, who believe in the lordship of Jesus Christ. I bless you for my faith, nourished in the Catholic Church, which has given me so much that is of value in my life. I regret the divisions and prejudices which have done much harm to the preaching and witness of the Christian gospel. Only you, Holy Spirit, can make us one. We pray for this in the holy name of Jesus.

M.B.

Prayer for Health and Care

Holy Spirit, teach us never to be afraid of finding out what is wrong in body, mind, or spirit. Ignorance is not bliss where health is concerned. We need to seek the skill of those who have dedicated their lives to caring for medical and emotional needs. We thank you for all doctors and nurses, and we pray that you will bless them as you give skill to their hands, discernment in their judgments, and compassion in their hearts. Open their eyes to the awareness that they are not dealing with just a mind or a body, but with a whole person. May they see in me and in all their patients the image of the wounded Christ.

M.B.

Slow Me Down

Holy Spirit, without you no prayer is possible. Because I am weakened by sin, there are 1,001 things that distract me so much that I sometimes lose the desire to pray. Prayer becomes a duty I have to fulfill, and so I get my prayers "in," prayers that are "just words" that do not flow from my heart.

Lord, slow me down and fill me with your presence as I listen to what you say to me today. My listening is much more important than anything I can say to you. So I ask you to encourage me to sit and listen to your still small voice when my world is hushed. Your peace is all I seek: This I know is my deepest prayer. Come, Holy Spirit, and slow me down.

M.B.

Thank You

Holy Spirit, I thank you for the gift of my faith in Jesus Christ, my Lord and Savior, and for the many blessings I have received from you.

I thank you for having placed me through no merit of

my own, in the holy Catholic Church, which has been for me a very powerful and unique way of living my faith to the full.

I thank you that Jesus came to earth as one of us and died so that in his resurrection we might share in his eternal life.

I thank you for all the special people in my life who enable me to receive your unique gift of experiencing a personal God as my Father.

I thank you that you are blessing other members of other churches with the grace of your life and presence. May more people come to know you as I have through my spiritual brothers and sisters in the church, which is Christ's body.

M.B.

When I Am Lonely

Holy Spirit, give me an awareness today of my heavenly Father's loving presence whenever I feel so alone that even my prayers are as dry and parched as an endless barren desert. May I find an oasis in your presence so that I do not feel the need to use words, because you are already there with and for me.

Give me the assurance to listen, the serenity to be still, and the faith to believe that all I am and feel in my barrenness is a prayer. Know that in lonely quiet places, I am more prepared to listen to my Father who loves and cares for me than to use words that may not express my dearest inner feelings. Teach me to be still and listen.

M.B.

Bless Us to Be ...

Holy Spirit, you were sent by God our Father and Christ
Jesus, his only Son, to be our Comforter, Counselor, and
Guide. Be with us this day and bless us so that we may be:
considerate to those less fortunate than ourselves,
joyful to those who have little in their lives to cheer them,
compassionate to those who have been cruelly treated by
    their family or friends,
generous to those in financial need that causes them
    undue worry and anxiety concerning themselves and
    those they love,
sympathetic to those who are hurting deep inside,
loving to those who feel that there is no such sincere emo-
    tion as unselfish love.

M.B.

May We Seek Your Guidance

Holy Spirit, be with us today in everything that we have to
do. May we never put off until tomorrow what we know
in our hearts we should do today. May we seek your guidance before we make any meaningful decision that will
affect our lives or others'. As we face up to problems, give
us wisdom, so our choices will bring peace and fulfillment
to everyone concerned. We pray that you will lighten any
darkness that surrounds us, so we may walk in honesty and
come to the day's end secure in the knowledge that you
have been with us, guiding and loving us.

M.B.

You Lead Me by a Light

Holy Spirit, you have been with me since my baptism. Yet how seldom do I raise my mind to your presence. Nonetheless, you are within me, forming and enlightening me in all the events of life when I freely let you do so. But you will not force yourself upon me; you lead me by a light and not by a chain. You call to my heart by the words of the Messiah, our Lord Jesus Christ. You strengthen me and form me by these mysterious words which shape me as the words of the Creator shaped the waste and void into the living earth. O Holy and Mysterious Spirit, I am so weak and so blind, so poor and so much in conflict with myself. Breathe on me, O Spirit, and I shall be renewed. Touch me with your grace and I shall be made whole again. Enlighten me and I shall see all that blinds me. Lift me and I shall run in the way of your commandments.

Benedict Groeschel, C.F.R.

Breathe on Me

Breathe on me, Breath of God,
Fill me with life anew....

Breathe on me, Breath of God,
Until my heart is pure,
Until with you I will one will,
To do and to endure.

Edwin Hatch

Part 5

WEDNESDAY:

LOVING
YOURSELF

INTRODUCTION

God our Father wants us to grow in an awareness and love of the person we are as we reach out in hope to the person we want to become. He gives us grace to achieve our potential, so that through our daily encounter with him in prayer and in people we become more fully human, fully alive, fully Christian.

True Christian love of self reflects Christ's love of his own humanity. He has chosen us to be his witnesses to the value of being fully human, fully alive. The Spirit also lives in us and fills us with an awareness of love which never comes to an end. Through the gift of love we reach out to God and our neighbor, so that we are fulfilled in this life and the next. True love of self is necessary for this relationship. In our prayer, while we are conscious of our own failings, we remind ourselves of God's love for us, which in turn helps us to love and forgive ourselves.

I Know He Prays for Me

I know that my Redeemer lives,
And ever prays for me;
A token of his love he gives,
A pledge of liberty.

Charles Wesley

King David's Prayer

Lord, you have searched me and you know
Where'er I rest, where'er I go,
You do know all that I have planned,
And all my ways are in your hand.

My words from you I cannot hide;
I feel your power on every side;
Oh, wondrous knowledge, awful might,
Unfathomed depth, unmeasured height.

Where can I go apart from you,
Or whither from your presence flee?
In heaven? It is your dwelling fair;
In death's abode? Lo, you are there.

If I the wings of morning take,
And far away my dwelling make,
The hand that leads me there is thine,
And my support your power divine.

Adapted from Psalm 139, The Psalter Hymnal

SCRIPTURE AND QUOTES FOR MEDITATION

Where the Spirit of the Lord is, there is freedom. And we, with our unveiled faces reflecting like mirrors the brightness of the Lord, all grow brighter and brighter as we are turned into the image that we reflect; this is the work of the Lord who is Spirit.

2 CORINTHIANS 3:18

Can you not buy two sparrows for a penny? And yet not one falls to the ground without your Father knowing. Why, every hair on your head has been counted. So there is no need to be afraid; you are worth more than hundreds of sparrows.

MATTHEW 10:29-31

For anyone who is in Christ, there is a new creation; the old creation has gone, and now the new one is here. It is all God's work. It was God who reconciled us to himself through Christ.

2 CORINTHIANS 5:17-18

You did not choose me,
no, I chose you.

JOHN 15:16

You are God's chosen race, his saints; he loves you.

COLOSSIANS 3:12

I have branded you on the palms of my hands.

ISAIAH 49:16

Do not be afraid, for I have redeemed you;
I have called you by your name, you are mine.

ISAIAH 43:1

Do not take fright, do not be afraid of them. Yahweh your
God goes ahead of you and will be fighting on your side,
just as you saw him act in Egypt. You have seen him in the
desert too: Yahweh your God continued to support you,
as a man supports his son, all along the road you followed
until you arrived here.

DEUTERONOMY 1:29-31, NJB

As the Father has loved me,
so I have loved you.
Remain in my love.
If you keep my commandments
you will remain in my love,
just as I have kept my Father's commandments
and remain in his love.
I have told you this
so that my own joy may be in you
and your joy be complete.

JOHN 15:9-11

Let us love one another,
since love is from God
and everyone who loves is a child of God and knows God.
Whoever fails to love does not know God,
because God is love.
This is the revelation of God's love for us,
that God sent his only Son into the world

that we might have life through him....
We have recognised for ourselves,
and put our faith in, the love God has for us.
God is love,
and whoever remains in love remains in God
and God in him.

1 JOHN 4:7-9, 16, NJB

In the abundance of his glory may he, through his Spirit,
enable you to grow firm in power with regard to your
inner self, so that Christ may live in your hearts through
faith, and then, planted in love and built on love, with all
God's holy people you will have the strength to grasp the
breadth and the length, the height and the depth; so that,
knowing the love of Christ, which is beyond knowledge,
you may be filled with the utter fullness of God.

Glory be to him whose power, working in us, can do
infinitely more than we can ask or imagine.

EPHESIANS 3:16-20, NJB

I am no longer trying for perfection by my own efforts,
the perfection that comes from the Law, but I want only
the perfection that comes through faith in Christ, and is
from God, and based on faith. All I want is to know Christ
and the power of his resurrection and to share his sufferings by reproducing the pattern of his death. That is the
way I hope to take my place in the resurrection of the
dead. Not that I have become perfect yet: I have not yet
won, but I am still running, trying to capture the prize for
which Christ Jesus captured me.

PHILIPPIANS 3:9-12

Though the will to do what is good is in me, the power to do it is not: the good thing I want to do, I never do; the evil thing which I do not want—that is what I do. But every time I do what I do not want to, then it is not myself acting, but the sin that lives in me....

What a wretched man I am! Who will rescue me from this body doomed to death? God—thanks be to him—through Jesus Christ our Lord.

ROMANS 7:18-20, 24, NJB

Those who live by their natural inclinations can never be pleasing to God. You, however, live not by your natural inclinations, but by the Spirit, since the Spirit of God has made a home in you. Indeed, anyone who does not have the Spirit of Christ does not belong to him. But when Christ is in you, the body is dead because of sin but the spirit is alive because you have been justified; and if the Spirit of him who raised Jesus from the dead has made his home in you, then he who raised Christ Jesus from the dead will give life to your own mortal bodies through his Spirit living in you.

ROMANS 8:8-11, NJB

Didn't you realize that you were God's temple and that the Spirit of God was living among you?

1 CORINTHIANS 3:16

Is there anyone who knows the qualities of anyone except his own spirit, within him; and in the same way, nobody knows the qualities of God except the Spirit of God. Now, the Spirit we have received is not the spirit of the world but

God's own Spirit, so that we may understand the lavish gifts God has given us.

1 CORINTHIANS 2:11-12, NJB

Men go forth to wonder at the height of mountains, the huge waves of the sea, the broad flow of the ocean, the course of the stars—and forget to wonder at themselves.

Saint Augustine

If you are yourself at peace, then there is at least *some* peace in the world. Then share your peace with everyone, and everyone will be at peace.

Thomas Merton

The glory of God is man, fully human, fully alive.

Saint Ireneaus

There is no seeming evil from which some soul of goodness may not be distilled.

William Shakespeare

Beware of despairing about yourself: you are commanded to put your trust in God, and not in yourself.

Saint Augustine

I am not what I ought to be;
I am not what I would like to be;
I am not what I hope to be.
But I am not what I once was,
and by the grace of God, I am what I am.

John Newton, author of "Amazing Grace"

Jesus and Me

O Lord,
never suffer us to think
that we can stand by ourselves,
and not need thee.

John Donne

The Heart of Mary

May I have the heart of Mary, empty of all and filled with
the All that is you.

George T. Montague, S.M.

Newman's Prayer

God has created me to do him some definite service.
He has committed some work to me which he has not
    committed to another.
I have my mission.
I may never know it in this life
But I shall be told it in the next.
I am a link in a chain.
A bond of connection between persons
He has not created me for naught
I shall do good—I shall do his work
I shall be an angel of peace
A preacher of truth in my own place
While not intending it
If I do but keep his commandments.
Therefore I will trust him
Whatever I am, I can never be blown away.
If I am in sickness, my sickness may serve him
In perplexity, my perplexity may serve him

If I am in sorrow, my sorrow may serve him
He does nothing in vain
He knows what he is about
He may take away my friends
He may throw me among strangers
He may make me feel desolate
Make my spirits sink
Hide my future from me—still
He knows what he is about.

John Henry Newman

Free Me From My Past
Dear Lord, free me from my dark past, into which I often find myself falling as if into a deep cistern…. Keep showing me your light, and give me the strength to rise and follow you without ever looking back.

Henri Nouwen

Creator Behind Our Creativity
We make, but thou art the creating core.
Whatever thing I dream, invent, or feel,
Thou art the heart of it, the atmosphere.
Thou art inside all love man ever bore;
Yea, the love itself, whatever thing be dear.

George Macdonald

May You Be Blessed Forever
May you be blessed forever, Lord, for loving me more than I love myself.

Saint Teresa of Avila

Be Nearer Me Than I Can Ask

This day be with me, Lord, when I go forth,
Be nearer to me than I am able to ask.
In merriment, in converse, or in task,
Walking the street, listening to men of worth,
Or greeting such as only talk and bask,
Be thy thought still my waiting soul around,
And if Christ come, I shall be watching found.

George Macdonald

A Steadfast Heart

Give me, O Lord, a steadfast heart which no unworthy thought can drag downwards; an unconquered heart which no tribulation can wear out; an upright heart which no unworthy purpose may tempt aside. Grant me also ... understanding to know you, diligence to seek you, wisdom to find you, and a faithfulness that may finally embrace you.

Saint Thomas Aquinas

Teach Me to Walk

Lord, teach me how to do your will,
And to walk worthily and humbly before you.
You are my wisdom; you know me well,
You knew me before the world was made
or ever I was born in it.

Thomas à Kempis

I Hunger and Thirst for You

Late have I loved you, O Beauty of ancient days, yet ever new; late have I loved you. And behold, you were within me and I was abroad, and there I searched for you.... You were with me, but I was not with you. Things held me far from you, things that would not have existed apart from you. You called, you shouted, you burst my deafness. You flashed, you shone, you scattered my blindness. You breathed fragrance and I drew in breath and panted for you. I tasted you, and now I hunger and thirst for you. You touched me, and I burned for your peace.

Saint Augustine

Send Your Healing Peace

God, you are a loving Father who wants to heal us and make us whole. Living in a world damaged by sin, we feel the pain of alienation from you, from our neighbor, and from what we ourselves should be. Be with us today in our suffering and send your healing peace into the midst of our pain. We cannot be or live at peace by our own unaided efforts, so send your Spirit upon us, so that we may know that you are with us. We offer to you all our sufferings in union with the loving obedience of Jesus your only Son, our Lord.

M.B.

Jesus, We Forget

Jesus, we forget so easily that life means more than food and the body more than clothing, and that you have invited us to look at the birds of the air flying so gracefully and freely. They are fed by their Creator, our heavenly

Father. Lord, when today we start feeling caged by worry and the stress of "success," fill us with faith, give us the courage to trust you and rest in the success that only you can give—the freedom of spirit that makes us soar.

M.B.

I Desire to Love You

Lord ... I desire to love you; I fear that I do not love you enough. Grant me the fullness of pure love. Behold my desire; you have given it to me. Behold in your creature what you have placed there. O God, who loves me enough to inspire me to love you forever, behold not my sins. Behold your mercy and my love.

Francois Fenelon

Your Love Heals Me

Father, you forgive my sins because you love me. I know that if I do not love myself for who and what I am, then I cannot love you. Sometimes the only reason I have for loving myself is that you, my Creator, love me. You do not love me because I am good and do your will in everything. You love and heal me because I am weak, and left to my own resources I would fail you in all that I am and do. You sent your Son, Jesus, to be the loving Doctor, who would heal my wounds. He is the Good Shepherd, who carries me as his wounded lamb on his shoulders because I would not have the strength to walk alone. Teach me today and every day to be determined to be strong and do your will. But when I fall, help me to remember that you love me still.

M.B.

Change Me

Heavenly Father, I know you have no favorites, and each person is special to you. You love me as I am today, and you are patient in waiting for me to change for the better because you want me to be free in willing and wanting to change. Loving Father, change me. In my weakness be my strength. In my false security be my challenge. In my lukewarmness be a fire within me. And in my life, which is in a rut, raise me up so I can really live and face the future with grace and gallantry.

M.B.

A Constant Prayer

My God, here I am, my heart devoted to you. Fashion me according to your heart.

Brother Lawrence

Trust in God

Father, as another day begins, I renew my trust in you. Because you love me as my Father, you will guide me along the right path, even though I may not be certain where it will lead. All I desire is to do your will throughout this day, and I trust that your Holy Spirit has placed this desire within me. Teach me to live one day at a time, and may I hope in you. Keep me joyful and at peace until the shadows lengthen and the day is done.

M.B.

Prayerful Life Creed

I would be true, for there are those who trust me;
I would be pure, for there are those who care;
I would be strong, for there is much to suffer;
I would be brave, for there is much to dare.

I would be friend of all, the foe, the friendless;
I would be giving, and forget the gift;
I would be humble, for I know my weakness;
I would look up, and laugh and love and lift.

I would be prayerful through each busy moment;
I would be constantly in touch with God;
I would be tuned to hear his slightest whisper;
I would have faith to keep the path Christ trod.

Howard Arnold Walter

The Gospel Speaks

Lord, your gospel is so meaningful that as I reflect on it this morning, I know that I will never fully understand the depths of your message that speaks to me deep within. Your words have many shades of meaning. You have colored your words with many hues, so that each person who studies them can see in them what he or she loves and a personal challenge to live a fuller Christian life. Thank you, Lord.

M.B.

Abundant Life

Lord Jesus, let me live this day to the full. Fill it with all the wonder and joy I knew as a child. Let me trust and welcome with an open mind and heart everyone I encounter today, so that this evening I may feel that I have contributed to the joy and peace of the world—this world that you entered so humbly and hopefully that we might have life to the full.

M.B.

May I Discover My True Self

Lord Jesus Christ, great Communicator with people and Lover of silence, help me to reflect on you deep within myself, so that with the noise of the busy work stilled I may in silence find you, and in finding you discover my true self.

M.B.

Respect for My Body

Lord Jesus, you were stripped naked in public and nailed to a cross. You turned that scene of shame into a triumph of love so that the crucifix is forever a sign of your victory over sin and evil. May I always respect my body as a gift given to me by my Father. May I always use food and drink for nourishment, neither eating nor drinking to excess nor eating too little and so damaging my body. May I never be ashamed of my body, realizing that my attitude toward this, your gift, is more important than anyone else's perception of how I look.

M.B.

Show Us How to Be Generous

Lord, show us how to be generous and not to count the cost. By the light of your wisdom, help us to follow our consciences and do what is right. May we find fulfillment as we face the challenges of this day with faith, trust, and generosity of spirit.

M.B.

Mindful of Your Love

Heavenly Father, help us today to be so mindful of your love and your will for us that we reflect it in everything we say and do. In our dealings with others, may we be gentle and forgiving, especially toward those who tend to irritate us. May nothing make us lose our temper, threaten our peace, or take away the joy of life, your gift to us. May we be cheerful even when we are disappointed, hopeful even when we face unexpected difficulties, and understanding of views that differ from our own. At the end of this day, may we know that through your grace we have been in some way a support to others, a credit to our professed Christian faith, and a source of glory and praise to you, our Father, through Christ our Lord.

M.B.

Help Us Keep Perspective

Father, may we rest our lives in you who know and provide for all our needs. May we keep our material goods in perspective, so that we never let our relationship with our loved ones get out of focus, so that we never endanger our deep inner peace and awareness that you love us as we are, and not for what we achieve by worldly standards.

M.B.

Shine Through Us Today

Father, Provider of all our needs, as we walk through life, help us today and always to remain secure in the knowledge that the only thing we need to carry into our eternal home is your love, which we pray will shine through us, as a witness to others with whom we share our pilgrimage.

M.B.

Teach Us to Use Our Gifts

Father, you know what is in us, our weaknesses and our strengths. Teach us through your loving-kindness and understanding to appreciate our real value in your eyes, so that we may learn to use more and more creatively the gifts you have given to us; in loving ourselves in a truly Christian way, may we know, love, and serve you better; and as we have been encouraged by you, may we do the same for others.

M.B.

Love of My Country

Father, you alone are the Source and Root of our being and fulfillment. I praise you for having planted me in my native land. May I take with me wherever I go what is best in my culture and tradition, so that I may be a messenger of harmony, peace, and the unity of all people—no matter what native land they have been planted in.

M.B.

Help Me Spread Your Love

Father, you love all of us equally and yet each of us uniquely. Today make me aware of that love, so I am able and willing to open my heart to all those who need your friendship as well as mine. May I help them to find your love and true Life and the purpose it brings.

M.B.

Give Us Confidence

Father, we all carry wounds and scars of life and we all need confidence if we are to love ourselves and achieve the purpose for which you made us. We need self-assurance if we are to "make our way." I thank you for the people who have encouraged me to see something of value in myself that has enabled me to face life with calmness and confidence.

Help those who have never recovered from the wounds made by their families. Send your Spirit into their minds and hearts, so that they will understand why family members have behaved the way they did. As your children, help us all to live in the present, confident that living life now is the best way to heal the unhappy memories of the past.

M.B.

Forgive My Faults

Father, I thank you for knowing and loving me better than I know myself and for allowing me to know myself better than others know me. Heal me, I pray, by making me better than they suppose. And forgive my faults, even the ones they do not know about, so that trusting in you I may become the person you would have me be.

M.B.

Broken Resolutions

Lord, I am forever making resolutions that I never seem able to fulfill. Despite my failings over the years, I have never given up hoping that tomorrow will be a better day. Put in my heart the determination I need to continue making resolutions and the courage to see them through so that one day they will become a reality.

M.B.

Perfect What Is Good

Father, whose mercy is boundless and whose gifts are without end, give me the courage to be myself and make me truly grateful that you have made me as I am. What is wrong in me, I ask you to help me change. Whatever is good in me, bring it to perfection. I pray this in faith and thank your holy name.

M.B.

Part 6

THURSDAY:

LOVING
YOUR
NEIGHBOR

INTRODUCTION

Christ has told us that the only way to learn to love God and ourselves is to love other people. If we want to have a deep inner peace with ourselves, we have to share ourselves with others. Christ, our Friend, gives us an example of generous love, which through his Spirit we seek to follow.

He chose followers whom he called friends to share his life and mission. In a special sense he was the friend of everyone and excluded no one, not even his enemies from his friendship. Unconditional love for others was to be for all time the essential mark of his church. By this unique love of our neighbors we would not only grow in the Christian life, but become in the process better and more fully human. Love for Christ whom we see in others is the greatest force for peace in the world, a peace that the world itself cannot give.

God's Residence
Who has not found the heaven below
   Will fail of it above.
God's residence is next to mine—
   His furniture is love.

                                 Emily Dickinson

SCRIPTURE AND QUOTES FOR MEDITATION

I give you a new commandment:
love one another;
just as I have loved you,
you also must love one another.
By this love you have for one another,
everyone will know that you are my disciples.

                                 JOHN 13:34-35

To disconcert [Jesus,] one of [the Pharisees] put a question, "Master, which is the greatest commandment of the Law?" Jesus said, "You must love the Lord your God with all your Heart, with all your soul, and with all your mind. This is the greatest and the first commandment. The second resembles it: You must love your neighbor as yourself. On these two commandments hang the whole Law, and the Prophets also."

                            MATTHEW 22:35-40

Anyone who claims to be in the light
but hates his brother
is still in the dark.
But anyone who loves his brother is living in the light
and need not be afraid of stumbling.

1 JOHN 2:9-10

You have heard how it was said, *You will love your neigh-*
bour and hate your enemy. But I say this to you, love your
enemies and pray for those who persecute you; so that you
may be children of your Father in heaven, for he causes his
sun to rise on the bad as well as the good, and sends down
rain to fall on the upright and the wicked alike. For if you
love those who love you, what reward will you get? Do not
even the tax collectors do as much? And if you save your
greetings for your brothers, are you doing anything exceptional? Do not even the gentiles do as much? You must
therefore be perfect, just as your heavenly Father is perfect.

MATTHEW 5:43-48, NJB

So from now on, there must be no more lies. *Speak the*
truth to one another, since we are all parts of one another.
Even if you are angry, do not sin: never let the sun set on
your anger or else you will give the devil a foothold.
Anyone who was a thief must stop stealing; instead he
must exert himself at some honest job with his own hands
so that he may have something to share with those in
need. No foul word should ever cross your lips; let your
words be for the improvement of others, as occasion
offers, and do good to your listeners; do not grieve the
Holy Spirit of God who has marked you with his seal,

ready for the day when we shall be set free. Any bitterness or bad temper or anger or shouting or abuse must be far removed from you—as must every kind of malice. Be generous to one another, sympathetic, forgiving each other as readily as God forgave you in Christ.

EPHESIANS 4:25-32, NJB

Believe me, it's a long apprenticeship, learning to love, ... Loving is always leaving oneself to go towards others.

Michel Quoist

The greatest thing a man can do for his heavenly Father is to be kind to some of his other children.

Henry Drummond

We cannot be sure if we are loving God, although we may have good reasons for believing that we are, but we can know quite well if we are loving our neighbor.

Saint Teresa of Avila

Trinitarian Blessing
May the grace of Christ our Savior
And the Father's boundless love,
With the Holy Spirit's favor,
Rest upon us from above.

Thus may we abide in union
With each other and the Lord,
And possess, in sweet communion,
Joys which earth cannot afford.

John Newton

Traditional Blessing for Friends

May the road rise to meet you.
May the wind be always at your back.
May the sun shine warm upon your face.
May the rain fall softly upon your fields.
Until we meet again,
May God hold you in the hollow of his hand.

Gaelic Blessing

Morning Prayer for a Friend

God, please grant her one fine day.
A cup of coffee alone with you.
A task to complete for your glory.
A ponderable thought.
A hearty laugh.
An affectionate hug.
An evensong.
A midnight prayer.

Evelyn Bence

Help Us to Build Each Other Up

Help us to help each other, Lord,
Each other's cross to bear;
Let each his friendly aid afford,
And feel his brother's care.

Help us to build each other up,
Our little stock improve;
Increase our faith, confirm our hope,
And perfect us in love.

Charles Wesley

Pardon for Christ's Sake
Praised be my Lord for all those who pardon one another
for his love's sake.

Saint Francis of Assisi

Give Me Strength to Help
If there be some weaker one,
Give me strength to help him on;
If a blinder soul there be,
Let me guide him nearer thee.

John Greenleaf Whittier

Prayer for Those in Danger
O Trinity of love and power,
Our brethren shield in danger's hour,
From rock and tempest, fire and foe,
Protect them wheresoe'er they go:
And ever let there rise to thee
Glad hymns of praise from land and sea.

William Whiting

Give Us Love
Gracious Spirit, Holy Ghost,
Taught by thee we covet most,
Of thy gifts at Pentecost,
Holy heavenly, love.

Love is kind and suffers long,
Love is meek and thinks no wrong,
Love than death itself more strong;
Therefore, give us love.

Prophecy will fade away,
Melting in the light of day;
Love will ever with us stay;
Therefore, give us love.
Faith and hope and love we see,
Joining hand in hand, agree,
But the greatest of the three,
And the best, is love.

Christopher Wordsworth

Prayer for Those Far From Home

Father, as I thank you this morning for the blessing of my home, may I remember that no one is a stranger to you and no one is ever far from your loving care. In your kindness watch over refugees and exiles—those separated from their loved ones, those who are homeless—and bring them safely to a place that feels like home. Help me always to show them your kindness and to see in them the image of your Son, who left his home to come to this our earthly home so that one day we share with him the delights of heaven.

M.B.

Prayer for the Poor

Lord, by your grace, let the poor seeing me be drawn to Christ and invite him to enter their homes and their lives.

Mother Teresa

Loving Parents

Lord Jesus, thank you for the example you gave regarding priorities in personal relationships, especially with parents. I think this morning of the time you heard that your

mother was anxious to speak with you; you pointed to
your disciples and said that they too were your family. You
loved your mother dearly, she was at one with you, and yet
in your ministry you had to be yourself to fulfill your life
mission. Lord, this shows me the need to be free from
parental demands so I can be the person you want me to
be and fulfill the mission to which you called me.

I pray for all parents who find it difficult to give their
children sufficient time and space in which to grow as individuals in their own right. And I remember those who feel
suffocated by their parents. May they not become frus-
trated and bitter but have courage to speak out in love to
those who try to bind them too tightly to themselves. I
thank you for my own freedom and for those who encouraged me to find it. Grant that by my life, based on your
example, I may help to inspire others to discover for themselves true Christian freedom.

M.B.

May They Know Your Love

Jesus, you said your followers must always love one another as you have loved them. I pray that all the rules and
directions of various Christian denominations may flow
from this pure, everlasting love. I thank you for Christians
whose lives have mirrored this love and encouraged me to
try to do the same. May no one feel excluded from this
love and may everyone know the depth of the love of God,
their heavenly Father, their sacrificial Savior. May I encourage them by my words and actions this day to believe in
this healing truth, which lifts them up and gives them
hope.

M.B.

For Those Without Work

Heavenly Father, your Word says that by the sweat of our brows we are to earn our daily bread. This morning I thank you that throughout the years you have given me the health, skill, opportunity, and motivation to provide for myself and my family.

In a spirit of gratitude and sympathy, I pray for those whose labor has never been sought; they stand idle at the marketplace. Call them out, Lord, for some task you want them to perform. Give them a sense of self-assurance and confidence as they begin a new life in which their value is recognized. Make our society more aware of their needs, so that corporate leaders think not so much of profit as of the dignity and rights of people to engage in work that fulfills the purpose for which they were created.

M.B.

For Those Suffering Rejection

Lord Jesus, you knew the pain of being deserted by those you called your friends. We all suffer the pain of rejection in one form or another. It is hardest to bear in marriage when the rejection comes from someone in whom we placed our most treasured hopes for sharing a life together. I pray today for all those whose love is not returned or is even spurned. May they come to understand their hurt and grow through it, so it does not fester as a reason for thinking less of themselves. Fill their thoughts not of the darkness of the pain of yesterday, but of the dawn of tomorrow in which they will continue their journey in search of friendship, peace, and fulfillment.

M.B.

To Recapture the Vision of Marriage

Lord Jesus, you saw life as a challenge. This is why you called Peter and his friends to leave everything behind them and follow you. It is the same with marriage, when a man and woman leave their separate homes to live together as one. But sometimes they lose their vision of what true marriage is all about; they lose their way, and their life together becomes meaningless.

Lord, help all married couples recapture today the vision of what their life together should be in you.

M.B.

Help Me Forgive My Enemies

Lord Jesus, you said I was to love my enemies. I have always found this difficult, especially when they treat me unjustly. I ask you, Lord, to put your mind and heart within me to learn to forgive them even though it is not now possible for me to forget, as I still bear scars in my spirit and emotions. Deepen in me a spirit of love and forgiveness that will overcome and dispel any thoughts of revenge or getting even. Be with me, Lord, this day as I think of you and how you suffered and forgave your enemies. Fill me with your presence and love, so there is no room in me for anything other than a spirit of goodwill and forgiveness toward everyone.

M.B.

Release Them From Hurtful Memories

Father, I thank you for my parents, brothers, sisters, and friends who nurtured me as I was growing up. In my gratitude for this blessing, I remember those today whose unhappy childhood still hurts them and limits their joy in living. I pray that they be released from the destructive pain of their hurtful memories, which shackles them to the past. May the love and friendship they now enjoy enable them to live in such a way that they are able to build up happy memories that will be a positive influence in their future and a source of healing.

M.B.

May They Be Good Parents
Father, from whom all fatherhood on earth comes, I give you thanks for my father and the hours he spent lovingly with me in my childhood. I pray that you will bless those who have never known a father's love; give them this day the grace to be the kind of parent to their children that they would have longed to have known themselves.

M.B.

Sharing Our Joys and Sorrows
Lord Jesus, you so loved being one of us that you showed us how valuable close friendships were for your growth and understanding of what it means to be human. In moments of great joy and deep pain, we discover who we really are, and it's so important that we share these experiences with those who are close to us.

The joy of a wedding feast at Cana, when you turned water into wine at your mother's request, did not prevent her standing at the foot of your cross as a soldier gave you vinegar to drink. Peter, James, and John, who were exhilerated when they saw you transfigured on Mount Tabor, your face shining like the sun and your clothes white as light, were also with you in the agony of Gethsemane, when your sweat became as drops of blood and you asked them to stay awake to keep you company.

Be with us, Lord, in our moments of great joy; grant us the grace and humility to share them with those we love, and through the sharing, may we come closer to one another and to you.

Teach us that we were not meant to live and die alone but as members of the human family, and that in sharing with others we are really sharing with you.

M.B.

Rejoice in the Gifts

Father, you have called your children to live as friends; may we encourage and rejoice in the gifts you have given to others, so that the darkness of jealousy never clouds our minds and keeps us from acknowledging that every gift comes from you, the Father of all.

M.B.

Heal Us Who Gather Together

Father, your Son Jesus Christ promised his special healing presence in the midst of two or three people gathered in his name. We thank you for the love your Spirit has poured out on our Christian community, so that together we share Christ's healing power and remain open to one another and to you who want to heal our relationships with you, with each other, and even with ourselves.

M.B.

Simple Witness

Father, Saint Francis admonished us to preach the gospel at all times; "if necessary use words." Your message of love is often best presented by those whose simple lifestyle empowers their words, making others aware of your care and concern. Teach us today and always to live simply and sincerely, letting our lifestyle be a witness to our Christian commitment to love and serve others as Christ would have us do.

M.B.

Prayer for a Grieving Friend

Father, look with pity on all those who walk in the valley of the shadow of death, surrounded by the memory of loved ones. Give them a lively faith in the resurrection of your Son, so that the expectation of a heavenly reunion gives them strength to live today—and tomorrow—with sweet memories and joyful hope. May the joy of the past with their loved ones be a foretaste of the future happiness that will never end.

M.B.

Prayer for Adoptive Homes

Father, you provided your Son Jesus with a loving home; bless all adopted children with a loving, caring family life. May the children be a source of happiness and fulfillment to their parents, and may the parents love and cherish the children as their very own.

M.B.

Help Me Be a Channel of Love

Father, give me a heart full of gratitude to you for all you have given to me and a serenity that nothing can disturb, so that in my daily contacts with others I may be to them a channel of your love, gentleness, and joy.

M.B.

None Can Live by Bread Alone

Heavenly Father, open our hearts to the poor and hungry. May we make friends with them. And in sharing bread with them, make us aware of our deep spiritual needs. And in making us aware of our spiritual hunger, help us to do all we can to relieve our community's spiritual hunger— knowing that none of us can live on bread alone.

M.B.

Beyond Prejudice

Father, when your Son lived in Palestine, many could not look beyond the fact that he came from the lowly town of Nazareth. Teach me to see beyond the human wrappings of those I meet. And, while stripping me of my prejudices, clothe us all in the beauty of your loving self in whose image we are all made.

M.B.

Bless Those Who Have Blessed Us

Father, bless all those whose influence, often unwittingly, has stirred our faith, renewed our hope, and rekindled our love, so that through them we have turned to you as the one true God who holds our lives in the palm of your hand.

M.B.

Make Me an Instrument

Lord, make me an instrument of your peace:
    where there is hatred, let me sow peace,
    where there is injury, let me sow pardon,
    where there is doubt, let me sow faith,
    where there is despair, let me give hope,
    where there is darkness, let me give light,
    where there is sadness, let me give joy.
O divine Master, grant that I may
    not try to be comforted but to comfort,
    not try to be understood but to understand,
    not try to be loved but to love.
Because it is in giving that we receive,
    it is in forgiving that we are forgiven,
    and it is in dying that we are born to eternal life.

Saint Francis of Assisi

Part 7

FRIDAY:

INNER
PEACE

INTRODUCTION

Inner peace is Christ's special gift to us. Without it we will never realize our potential as Christians and be truly happy. Being damaged by sin, we are often victims of irrational fear, guilt, unnecessary tension, despondency, depression, hurtful memories, lack of purpose, and numerous other negatives that prevent us from being fully human, fully Christian. We need God's loving help and encouragement if we are to break the bonds that fetter and limit our lives.

In our prayers we face up to weaknesses within ourselves, and with the power of the Holy Spirit we conquer them and learn to walk in peace with ourselves and our neighbors.

Inner peace for many people is a word which trips lightly off the tongue without ever penetrating their mind and heart. We do not understand its deep significance or the changes it calls for in our way of life. Peace costs nothing less than everything, and in prayer we ask for the courage to become peacemakers within ourselves and with others. Christ alone is the peace between us.

SCRIPTURE AND QUOTES FOR MEDITATION

Peace I bequeath to you,
my own peace I give you,
a peace the world cannot give, this is my gift to you.
Do not let your hearts be troubled or afraid.

JOHN 14:27

Do not worry; do not say, "What are we to eat? What are we to drink? How are we to be clothed?" It is the pagans who set their hearts on all these things. Your heavenly Father knows you need them all. Set your hearts on his kingdom first, and on his righteousness, and all these other things will be given you as well. So do not worry about tomorrow: tomorrow will take care of itself. Each day has enough trouble of its own.

MATTHEW 6:31-34

[Jesus] got into the boat followed by his disciples. Suddenly a storm broke over the lake, so violent that the boat was being swamped by the waves. But he was asleep. So they went to him and woke him saying, "Save us, Lord, we are lost!" And he said to them, "Why are you so frightened, you who have so little faith?" And then he stood up and rebuked the winds and the sea; and all was a great calm.

MATTHEW 8:23-26, NJB

Though they had been present when [Jesus] gave so many signs, they did not believe in him....

And yet there were many who did believe in him, even among the leading men, but they did not admit it, because of the Pharisees and for fear of being banned from the synagogue: they put human glory before God's glory.

JOHN 12:37, 42-43, NJB

When [your enemies] lead you away to hand you over, do not worry beforehand about what to say; no, say whatever is given to you when the time comes, because it is not you who will be speaking: it will be the Holy Spirit.

MARK 13:11

I want you to be happy, always happy in the Lord; I repeat, what I want is your happiness. Let your tolerance be evident to everyone: the Lord is very near. There is no need to worry; but if there is anything you need, pray for it, asking God for it with prayer and thanksgiving, and that peace of God, which is so much greater than we can understand, will guard your hearts and your thoughts, in Christ Jesus.

PHILIPPIANS 4:4-7

I know how to be poor and I know how to be rich too. I have been through my initiation, and now I am ready for anything anywhere: full stomach or empty stomach, poverty or plenty. There is nothing I cannot master with the help of the One who gives me strength.

PHILIPPIANS 4:12-13

I have told you all this
so that you may find peace in me.
In the world you will have trouble,
but be brave:
I have conquered the world.

JOHN 16:33

Can anything cut us off from the love of Christ—can hardships or distress, or persecution, or lack of food and clothing, or threats or violence...? No; we come through all these things triumphantly victorious, by the power of him who loved us.

For I am certain of this: neither death nor life, nor angels, nor principalities, nothing already in existence and nothing still to come, nor any power, nor the heights nor the depths, nor any created thing whatever, will be able to come between us and the love of God, known to us in Christ Jesus our Lord.

ROMANS 8:35, 37-39, NJB

In the meantime, brothers, we wish you happiness; try to grow perfect; help one another. Be united; live in peace, and the God of love and peace will be with you.

2 CORINTHIANS 13:11

Yahweh is my light and my salvation,
     whom need I fear?
Yahweh is the fortress of my life,
     of whom should I be afraid?
When evil men advance against me
     to destroy my flesh,

they, my opponents, my enemies,
  are the ones who stumble and fall....

Never leave me, never desert me,
  God my saviour!
If my father and mother desert me,
  Yahweh will care for me still....

This I believe: I shall see the goodness of Yahweh,
  in the land of the living.
Put your hope in Yahweh, be strong, let your heart be
  bold, put your hope in Yahweh.

PSALM 27:1-2, 9-10, 13-14

I seek Yahweh, and he answers me,
frees me from all my fears.

PSALM 34:4, NJB

Trust in Yahweh and do what is good,
make your home in the land and live in peace;
make Yahweh your only joy
and he will give you what your heart desires.

Commit your fate to Yahweh,
trust in him and he will act.

PSALM 37:3-5

My guilt is overwhelming me,
it is too heavy a burden;
my wounds stink and are festering,
the result of my folly;

bowed down, bent double, overcome,
I go mourning all the day....

Yes, I admit my guilt,
I am sorry for having sinned....

Yahweh, do not desert me,
do not stand aside, my God!
Come quickly to my help,
Lord, my saviour!

PSALM 38:3-6, 18, 21-22

Do not be afraid to throw yourself on the Lord. He will
not draw back and let you fall. Put your worries aside and
throw yourself on him: He will welcome you and heal you.
Saint Augustine

In "pastures green"? Not always; sometimes he
Who knows best, in kindness leads me
In weary ways where heavy shadows be.
Out of the sunshine warm and soft and bright,
Out of the sunshine into darkest night.
I oft would faint with sorrow and affright,
Only for this I know he holds my hand.
So whether in a green or desert land,
I trust him, though I do not understand.

And "by still waters"? No, not always so;
Oft times the heavy tempests round me blow,
And o'er my soul the waves and billows go.
But when the storm beats loudest, and I cry

Aloud for help, the Master stands by
And whispers to my soul, "Lo! It is I."
Above the wildest wild I hear him say,
"Beyond this darkness lies the perfect day,
In every path of thine I lead the way."

So whether on the hilltop high and fair
I dwell, or in the sunless valley where
The shadows lie—what matter? He is there.
Yea more than this: Where'er the pathway lead
He gives to me no helpless broken reed,
But his own hand sufficient for my need.
So where he leads me, I can safely go,
And in the blest hereafter I shall know
Why, in his wisdom, he has led me so.

Author Unknown

Peace, perfect peace, with loved ones far away?
In Jesus' keeping we are safe and they.

Edward Bickersteth

Blessing
The wisdom of the wonderful Counselor guide you. The strength of the mighty God defend you. The love of the everlasting Father enfold you. The peace of the Prince of Peace be upon you. And the blessing of God almighty, Father, Son, and Holy Spirit be upon you all now and ever more.

Author Unknown

Our Days Are Numbered

Our days are numbered: let us spare
Our anxious hearts a needless care:
'Tis yours to number out our days;
'Tis ours to give them to your praise.

Madame Jeanne Guyon

Daily Prayer

Grant that I may live my days calmly and fully.

Michel Quoist

The Dew of Quietness

Drop your still dews of quietness,
Till all our strivings cease;
Take from our souls the strain and stress,
And let our ordered lives confess
The beauty of your peace.

John Greenleaf Whittier

Serenity

Grant me the serenity
to accept the things I cannot change,
the courage to change the things I can,
and the wisdom to distinguish the one from the other.

Reinhold Niebuhr

Teresa's Bookmark

Let nothing disturb thee,
Nothing affright thee;
All things are passing;

God never changeth;
Patient endurance
Attaineth to all things;
Who God possesseth
In nothing is wanting;
Alone God sufficeth.

Saint Teresa of Avila,
trans. by Henry Wadsworth Longfellow

Grant Us Peace

Grant us thy peace—that like a deepening river swells ever outward to a sea of praise.

Eliza Scudder

Source of Calm Repose

Thou hidden Source of calm repose,
Thou all-sufficient Love divine,
My help and refuge from my foes,
Secure I am while thou art mine;
And lo, from sin and grief and shame,
I hide me, Jesus, in thy name.

Charles Wesley

For Stillness and Inner Peace

Holy Spirit, I offer myself to your work of healing, peace, and reconciliation. In my busy world, bless my silent moments. In the stillness of my heart, may I find peace within myself, peace with others, and peace with you.

M.B.

May Guile Depart

May faith, deep rooted in the soul,
Subdue our flesh, our minds control;
May guile depart, and discord cease,
And all within be joy and peace.

Saint Ambrose

Prayer for Those Tortured by Guilt

Father, I pray this morning for all those so tortured by
guilt that they have rarely known a day's peace. May they
know you today as a loving God who heals all their ills and
removes their guilt as far away as the east is from the west.

M.B.

Peace of Forgiveness

Lord Jesus, I thank you that you gave your apostles the
power to forgive sins in your name and reconcile sinners to
your Father, their neighbors, and themselves. Though I
often have told you how sorry I am, yet I still persist in my
waywardness. I ask you, Lord, in your goodness to continue to forgive my failings in the future, and set my mind
at rest about my past. When you were on earth, you readily forgave sinners and encouraged them to live better lives.
I pray that today you will do the same for me, so that I live
in peace in my spirit, because I know that the abundance
of your love makes up for my lack of sorrow.

M.B.

May This Day Be Like Christmas

Lord Jesus, you came to earth for everyone so that no one would be excluded from your all-embracing love. Inspire me with the same spirit of generosity, so that I may always remain open, especially to those who have hurt me or toward whom I have nurtured resentment. May this, and every day, be like Christmas as you inspire me to bring peace and reconciliation to everyone I meet.

M.B.

Peace With Deceased Family

Father, from whom all fatherhood comes, forgive me for my lack of love for my earthly father who seemed so incapable of loving me like you, my perfect heavenly Father. Help me throughout this day to remember all the good times I shared with him, so that I may understand him better. He's no longer here for me to talk to. I wish I could have told him I loved him before he died. May I be consoled with the thought that when we meet in heaven, we will both experience love for each other in a new and beautiful way.

M.B.

Peace in Our World

Holy Spirit, I pray today for peace in our world and an end to violence. May there be peace in our homes and hearts so that we may live and work together in a spirit of peace and harmony. Remind me that I share my world with others, many less fortunate than I am and maybe resentful. Help me to understand their frustration, which often expresses itself in violence and anger. Purify the minds and attitudes of men and women in leadership, especially in the media, so that they present a better, more peaceful view of our world, rather than the violent image that agitates those troubled in spirit. May the world know Christ's peace, without which society loses its direction and ignores our deep desire for peace.

M.B.

Every Day in Peace

Lord Jesus Christ, you told us not to worry or be anxious; each day has enough troubles of its own; we are not to burden ourselves with memories of yesterday's problems or tomorrow's possible difficulties. Give me then a mind at rest, knowing that my Father is sensitive to all my needs for which he will provide. Place in my mind the conviction that I do not face any obstacle alone, because you are with me to give strength to my spirit. Tomorrow will look after itself, and yesterday is in your merciful care, because you have already taken it to yourself. So having nothing to fear, I shall with your help live this day, and all the days of my life, in your peace.

M.B.

Gift of Serenity

Lord Jesus, a peace which the world cannot give is your gift to your followers. Fill my mind and heart with your peace, so that I may look at the world through your eyes, and know that your precious gift keeps me serene no matter how turbulent my surroundings.

M.B.

Lessons of Peace

Lord, teach me to discern the peace I should seek, the peace I should keep, and the peace I should share.

M.B.

Seeing Others as Friends

Lord, peace means loving myself so that I am at peace in every situation. Today and every day, may I see everyone as a possible friend and not a potential enemy. As your peace comes to me, like gentle rain or sunshine, so may my peace flow out to others and nourish them so that they grow through your gift of peace.

M.B.

May I See Fear as My Enemy

Father, fear is the enemy of my personal freedom and growth in inner peace. Fearful people go through life growing old but never growing up. I am afraid, Father, of being afraid, because it diminishes and destroys my love for you and myself. Send your love into my heart, because only your perfect love can cast out my fear. May I see fear as my enemy, and with your help may I confront all my hidden fears.

M.B.

You Come to Our Aid

Father, in the midst of our troubles, you come to our aid. You do not help us before we have helped ourselves, but when we think we are at the end of our resources and cannot bear our burdens anymore, you lift us up, and then with you and because of you our courage and strength are renewed. Thank you, Lord, for coming to our aid.

M.B.

May I Be a Peacemaker

Lord Jesus, you know that even though the future is hidden from our eyes, our attitude today can influence our tomorrows. Help us to live in peace, so that future generations will find no cause in us for widening divisions or fostering violence. By our words and actions, may we be true peacemakers so that we can be called children of God our Father.

M.B.

May Goodwill Reign

Father, to announce the birth of your Son, you sent angels to sing of peace on earth to all those of goodwill. May the Spirit of Christ come again into the minds and hearts of all those living in the midst of violence. May people at peace hold fast to the goodwill that unites them. And may warring enemies forget their hatred and listen to the message of peace. Help me to be at peace in my mind and heart so that through your power it may spread to everyone I meet. May no word or action of mine disturb their peace or mine.

M.B.

Put Your Rest in My Mind

God, my Father, I turn to you in my unrest, because I cannot see any way out of the present troublesome conflict. In my confusion, I turn to you for help and guidance, because you alone can help me, and nothing is impossible to you. Light up my life with faith, and give me the courage to walk confidently where you would lead me.

You know the right time to lift the burden that oppresses me, and so I place the present moment, as I do my whole life, in your tender care. Put your rest in my mind, and your peace in my heart.

M.B.

Rest in Heaven

Bring us, O Lord our God, at our last awakening into the house and gate of heaven, to enter into that gate and dwell in that house, where there shall be no darkness or dazzling, but one equal light; no noise or silence, but one equal music; no fears or hopes, but one equal possession; no ends or beginnings, but one equal eternity; in the habitations of your glory and dominion, world without end.

John Donne

Poetic Peace

The Lord's my shepherd, I'll not want.
He makes me down to lie.
In pastures green, he leadeth me
The quiet waters by.
My soul he doth restore again,
And me to walk doth make
Within the paths of righteousness
E'en for his own name's sake.
Yea, though I walk in death's dark vale
Yet will I fear none ill.
For thou art with me, and thy rod
And staff me comfort still.

My table thou has furnished
In presence of my foes.
My head thou dost with oil anoint,
And my cup overflows.
Goodness and mercy all my life
Shall surely follow me,
And in God's house for evermore
My dwelling place shall be.

PSALM 23, Scottish Psalter

Part 8

SATURDAY:

OUR LADY
AND THE
SAINTS

INTRODUCTION

We honor Mary because she was chosen by God the Father as the mother of his only Son. We think of Mary in terms of the birth of our Lord. But that is only one part of her story. Dying on the cross, Jesus gave his mother, Mary, to us as our spiritual mother. She is the Mother of the church and Mother of all Christians. She was with the apostles and the holy women who prayed daily in the Upper Room until the Holy Spirit came upon them at Pentecost. She together with the saints and all the Christians who have gone before us pray that we too one day may be with them as together we praise the blessed Trinity.

In their lives on earth, the saints lived out the beatitudes preached by Jesus in his Sermon on the Mount. They are the models whose lives we should imitate so that like them we may witness to the power of the Holy Spirit at work in all ages and peoples. In prayer, as we praise God's grace manifest in them, we also pray for a deeper personal commitment to Christ and his church.

God of Saints

God of saints, to whom the number
Of the starry host is known:
Many saints by earth forgotten
Live forever round your throne.

There are named the blessed faithful
Of the new Jerusalem.
When Christ comes again in glory,
Number us, we pray, with them.

John Ellerton

SCRIPTURE AND QUOTES FOR MEDITATION

God said to the serpent, ...
"I will make you enemies of each other:
you and the woman,
your offspring and her offspring.
It will crush your head
and you will strike its heel."

GENESIS 3:14-15

Now a great sign appeared in heaven: a woman adorned
with the sun, standing on the moon, and with the twelve
stars on her head for a crown.

REVELATION 12:1

The Lord himself, therefore,
will give you a sign.
It is this: the maiden is with child
and will soon give birth to a son
whom she will call Immanuel.

ISAIAH 7:14

The angel Gabriel was sent by God to a town in Galilee called Nazareth, to a virgin betrothed to a man named Joseph, of the House of David; and the virgin's name was Mary.... The angel said to her, "Mary, do not be afraid.... You are to conceive and bear a son, and you must name him Jesus."... Mary said to the angel, "But how can this come about, since I am a virgin?" "The Holy Spirit will come upon you," the angel answered, "and the power of the Most High will cover you with its shadow. And so the child will be holy and will be called Son of God."

LUKE 1:26-27, 31, 34-35

My soul does magnify the Lord,
My spirit rejoices greatly
In God my Savior and his word;
For he has seen the low degree
Of me his handmaiden truly.
Behold now, after this day,
All generations shall speak of me,
And call me blessed always.
For he that is only of might
Has done great things for me;
And holy is his name by right:
As for his endless mercy,
It endures perpetually,
In every generation,
On them that fear him.

LUKE 1:46-50, COVERDALE

The time came for [Mary] to have her child, and she gave birth to a son, her first-born. She wrapped him in swaddling clothes, and laid him in a manger because there was no room for them at the inn.

LUKE 2:6-7

Simeon blessed them and said to Mary [Jesus'] mother, "Look, he is destined for the fall and for the rise of many in Israel, destined to be a sign that is opposed—and a sword will pierce your own soul too—so that the secret thoughts of many may be laid bare."

LUKE 2:34-35, NJB

Mary kept all these things, and pondered them in her heart.

LUKE 2:19, KJV

Now as [Jesus] was speaking, a woman in the crowd raised her voice and said, "Happy the womb that bore you and the breasts you sucked!" But he replied, "Still happier those who hear the word of God and keep it!"

LUKE 11:27-28

There was a wedding at Cana in Galilee.... The mother of Jesus said to him, "They have no wine." Jesus said "Woman, why turn to me? My hour has not come yet." His mother said to the servants, "Do whatever he tells you."... Jesus said to the servants, "Fill the jars with water," and they filled them to the brim. "Draw some out now," he told them, "and take it to the steward." They did this; the steward tasted the water, and it had turned into wine.

JOHN 2:1, 3-5, 7-9

[Jesus said,] "Anyone who does the will of my father in heaven, he is my brother and sister and mother."

MATTHEW 12:50

Near the cross of Jesus stood his mother.... Seeing his mother and the disciple whom he loved standing near her, Jesus said to his mother, "Woman, this is your son." Then to the disciple he said, "This is your mother." And from that hour the disciple took her into his home.

JOHN 19:25-27, NJB

On the Feast of the Annunciation I saw the heart of the Virgin Mother so bathed by the rivers of grace flowing out of the blessed Trinity that I understood the privilege Mary has of being the most powerful after God the Father, the most wise after God the Son, and the most kindly after God the Holy Spirit.

Saint Gertrude the Great

Mary's "yes" is a free responsible "yes" by which she accepts being the vessel of the creation to be embraced by her son Jesus. It is not the yes of self-denial, almost of irresponsibility, as it has been traditionally presented to us. Mary knows to whom she is committing herself.

Anna Maria Bidegain

There is nothing more wonderful than the life of Jesus in Mary, the holy life that he pours continuously into her, the divine life with which he animates her, loving and praising and adoring God the Father in her.

Jean-Jacques Olier

The bush seen by Moses which burnt without being consumed was a real symbol of Mary's heart.

Thomas of Villanova

Mother Mary

O Mother Maid! O Maid and Mother free!
O bush unburnt; burning in Moses' sight!
That down did ravish from the Deity,
Through humbleness, the spirit that did alight
Upon thy heart, whence, through that glory's might,
Conceived was the Father's sapience,
Help me to tell it in thy reverence.
Lady! Thy goodness, thy magnificence,
Thy virtue, and thy great humility,
Surpass all science and all utterance.

Geoffrey Chaucer, trans. by William Wordsworth

O Splendid Gem

O most splendid gem! The serene beauty of the sun is poured into you, the fountain springing from the heart of the Father, which is the only begotten Word, through whom he created the primary material of the world, which Eve troubled. He made this Word man in you, and you are that brilliant gem, from whom that Word brought forth all the virtues and in that primary matter produced all creatures.

Saint Hildegard of Bingen

Let Us Shelter Christ

Mother of Christ, Mother of Christ,
Come with thy Babe to me;
Though the world be cold, my heart shall hold
A shelter for him and for thee.

A Notre Dame Hymn

Hail, Holy Queen

Hail, holy Queen, Mother of mercy! Hail, our life, our sweetness and our hope. To thee do we cry, poor banished children of Eve; to thee do we send up our sighs, mourning and weeping in this vale of tears. Turn, then, most gracious advocate, thine eyes of mercy toward us, and after this our exile, show unto us the blessed fruit of thy womb, Jesus. O clement, O loving, O sweet Virgin Mary.

Pray for us, O holy Mother of God.

That we may be made worthy of the promises of Christ.

Traditional

The Memorare

Remember, O most loving Virgin Mary, that never was it known that anyone who fled to your protection, implored your help, or sought your intercession was left unaided. Inspired by this confidence, we fly unto you, O Virgin of virgins, our Mother! To you we come, before you we stand, sinful and sorrowful. O Mother of the Word incarnate, despise not our petitions, but in your mercy hear and answer us.

Traditional

Our Lady of Perpetual Succour

Most holy Virgin Mary, who, to inspire me with boundless confidence, has been pleased to take that name, Mother of Perpetual Succour, I beseech you to aid me at all times and in all places; in my temptations, in my difficulties, in all the miseries of life, and, above all, at the hour of my death so that I may share in the resurrection of your Son our Lord Jesus Christ.

Grant, most charitable Mother, that I may remember you at all times, and always have recourse to you; for I am sure that, if I am faithful in invoking you, you will promptly come to my aid. Obtain for me, therefore, the grace to pray to you unceasingly with filial confidence, and that, by virtue of this constant prayer, I may obtain your perpetual help and persevere in the practice of my faith. Bless me, most tender Mother, ever ready to aid me, and pray for me now and at the hour of my death.

Mother of Perpetual Succour, protect also all those whom I recommend to you, the church, the holy father, our country, my family, my friends and enemies, especially all those who suffer.

Traditional

The Angelus

The angel of the Lord declared unto Mary.
And she conceived by the Holy Spirit.
Hail Mary....

Behold the handmaid of the Lord.
Be it done unto me according to thy word.
Hail Mary....

And the Word was made flesh, and dwelt among us.
Hail Mary....

Pray for us, O holy Mother of God.
That we may be made worthy of the promises of Christ.

Let us pray. Pour forth, we beseech you, O Lord, thy grace into our hearts, that we, to whom the incarnation of Christ thy Son was made known by the message of an angel, may be brought, by his passion and cross, to the glory of his resurrection. Through the same Christ our Lord.

Traditional

Regina Coeli (said during Pascal time)
O Queen of heaven, rejoice, alleluia!
For he whom thou didst merit to bear, alleluia!
Has risen, as he said, alleluia!
Pray for us to God, alleluia!

Rejoice and be glad, O Virgin Mary, alleluia!
For the Lord has risen indeed, alleluia!

Let us pray. O God, who gavest joy to the world through the resurrection of thy Son our Lord Jesus Christ; grant that we may obtain, through his Virgin Mother, Mary, the joys of everlasting life. Through the same Christ our Lord.

Traditional

Thanking God for Mary

Heavenly Father, we praise and thank you for choosing Mary to be the mother of your Son Jesus and for placing him to her tender loving care. We praise you that he, growing up as child in home, knew from experience what being human really meant.

We know he understands our situation, because he was like us in everything but sin. He was not ashamed to ask a Samaritan woman for a drink of water when he was thirsty or to sleep in a storm-tossed boat when he was sleepy. He knew friendship and joy and sadness and every emotion, even to the pain of rejection that led to his crucifixion. And in his suffering his mother never left his side.

In thanking you for Jesus, we thank you also for Mary his mother. May we know and love her more, because in doing so, we will come closer to you and your Son Jesus Christ.

M.B.

A Mother's Loving Care

Mary our Mother, as Jesus' mother you experienced so many emotions that you are as close to us as you were to him. We pray that we may be as sensitive to the needs of others as you were at the wedding feast of Cana. Help us to enter into the minds and hearts of others, so that we may see things through their eyes.

We are all people wounded by sin, and we need a mother's loving, healing care. On the cross Jesus gave you to us, and we come to you in love, hope, and trust. Be a mother to us—better than any mother we have known here on earth. Mary our mother and queen, be with us today and always.

M.B.

We Need a Mother

Mary, the world needs a mother's love. Be with those this day who are always taken for granted and are never praised or encouraged. Heal those who have been hurt by lack of love and loyalty. Bless those who are especially lonely because a loved one is no longer with them. Bless those who are worried financially. Be a friend and mother to those who are afraid to reach out to others—afraid of being hurt. God the Father gave his Son into your care, and Jesus in turn made you the mother of his family, the church. Be with us this day and at the hour of our death.

M.B.

We Want to Live as She Did

God our Father, you blessed your church and world with the example of Mary, the mother of Jesus. We want to live as she did, and we know we cannot do it without the help of your Holy Spirit. We pray that, like her, we may never deliberately or insensitively hurt the feelings of others. May we never be jealous or condemnatory of others. Give us her heart, that we may forgive those who have offended us, even those we love. Grant that we may experience her deep inner peace, which heals us and makes us more human, happy, and alive.

M.B.

Prayer for Our Children

Mary, blessed mother of Jesus, help us to understand our children, so that like your Son they may grow in love and wisdom. By your example with your family in Nazareth, teach us to respect the great gift of human life that God our Father has committed to our care. Help us to listen with loving patience to our children's worries and problems. Give us tolerance to allow them to develop as individuals as Jesus did in your loving care.

M.B.

Mary Our Model

Mary, you have taught us to treasure family life and to fill it with unselfish love. Help us to imitate you, so that we see your Son Jesus not only in our own children but in every child we meet this day. May those who feel unwanted and unloved find in us the warm family love they yearn for but have never experienced. Like you, may we stand by their cross of loneliness and suffering and encourage them to hope for a better tomorrow where your Son's resurrection will brighten the darkness of their lives.

M.B.

Saint Godric's Morning Prayer

Holy Mary, Virgin clean,
Mother of the Nazarene,
Me, your Godric, help today.
Shield me, hear me, when I pray,
That with you eternally
In God's kingdom I may be.

Saint Godric

SCRIPTURE AND QUOTES FOR MEDITATION

Only faith can guarantee the blessings that we hope for, or prove the existence of realities that are unseen. It is for their faith that our ancestors are acknowledged....

These were men who through faith conquered kingdoms, did what was upright and earned the promises. They could keep a lion's mouth shut, put out blazing fires and emerge unscathed from battle. They were weak people who were given strength to be brave in war and drive back foreign invaders. Some returned to their wives from the dead by resurrection; and others submitted to torture, refusing release so that they would rise again to a better life. Some had to bear being pilloried and flogged, or even chained up in prison. They were stoned, or sawn in half, or killed by the sword; they were homeless, and wore only the skins of sheep and goats; they were in want and hardship, and maltreated. They were too good for the world and they wandered in deserts and mountains and in caves and ravines. These all won acknowledgement through their faith....

With so many witnesses in a great cloud all around us, we too, then, should throw off everything that weighs us down and the sin that clings so closely.

HEBREWS 11:1-2, 33-39; 12:1, NJB

[The Lord says:]
I am he who made all saints;
I gave them my good influence,
I showed them glory,

I called them by my favor,
I drew them by my pity,
I led them on through many a temptation,
I poured upon them wondrous consolations,
I gave them strength unto the end,
I crowned their suffering,
I know them first and last,
I throw my arms, with love past telling, around them,
I must be praised in all my saints.

Thomas à Kempis

For the Help of the Saints

May holy Mary, and all the saints, intercede this day for us with the Lord that we may be helped and protected by him who lives and reigns forever and ever.

M.B.

To Saint Joseph Our Teacher

May Saint Joseph become for all of us an exceptional teacher in the service of Christ's saving mission, a mission which is the responsibility of each and every member of the Church: husbands and wives, parents, those who live by the work of their hands or by any other kind of work, those called to the contemplative life, and those called to the apostolate.

This just man, who bore within himself the entire heritage of the Old Covenant, was also brought into the beginning of the New and Eternal Covenant in Jesus Christ. May he show us the paths of this saving Covenant as we stand at the threshold of the next millennium, in which there must be a continuation and further development of the "fullness of time" that belongs to the ineffable mystery of the Incarnation of the Word.

May Saint Joseph obtain for the church and for the world, as well as for each of us, the blessing of the Father, Son, and Holy Spirit.

Pope John Paul II

The Church for All Time

Lord Jesus, I praise and thank you this morning that you share your life completely, not only with your mother and all who followed you during your life on earth, but also with all those who until the end of time believe in your life, resurrection, and divinity. We are members of an extended family, the church, which reaches back to the first Christians and into the future and embraces all those who acclaim Jesus as their Lord and Leader.

The saints were good and holy people who have gone before us and have suffered much for their faith in you. They are our models and inspiration, and they ceaselessly pray for us that we will not be lacking in our commitment to you and one another. Through your extended family, time and eternity are linked in a unique way, so that no matter what trials and tribulations we endure, we believe that we never walk alone.

As this day begins, remind us that as members of your church we share in a special way with each other and with you, because you shared with us when you became human for our sake.

M.B.

Living Today With the Saints

Heavenly Father, Creator of the universe, as you draw back the veil that covers the light of day, grant that throughout our waking hours we may always remember that we are part of a huge cavalcade of holy people who through their lives gave witness to their belief that you were their Father. May we join with them as we live out the gospel of Jesus Christ in every situation in which we find ourselves today.

M.B.

Praying With the Saints

Father, remind us this day that we never pray alone, for you have given us the company and friendship of the saints who will take all our prayers to you. Whatever we ask for is echoed by a chorus of holy men and women who today reflect your glory as they behold you face to face. We thank you that all our prayers are assumed into this holy family and that for their sakes, as well as ours, you will answer them.

M.B.

The Vision of the Saints

Holy Spirit, today we remember how you inspired the saints down through the centuries with your vision, insight, and wisdom greater than any human understanding or knowledge. The prophet foretold of you:

> I shall pour out my spirit on all humanity.
> Your sons and daughters shall prophesy,
> and your old people shall dream dreams,
> and your young people see visions (Jl 3:1, NJB).

Saint Peter said this prophecy was fulfilled at Pentecost. The holy people, young and old, whom you inspired have been the saints whose lives bore witness to the message of Jesus Christ by sharing their dreams and visions with us. Enable us to make their dreams come true in our world and time in the name and for the sake of Jesus.

M.B.

The Example of the Saints

Father, we live in a world damaged by sin, and every day I am reminded of my weaknesses and failings. Like Saint Paul, I am only too well aware that I will to do what is good, yet I do not do what I want to do. May I keep before me this day the example of holy people like the saints who, despite the most harrowing sufferings and temptations, won the battle with their wounded selves and claimed the ultimate victory through Christ your Son.

M.B.

The Saints I Have Met

Holy Spirit, in my lifetime I have seen your gentle power at work in many people who to me are saints and whose Christian faith, hope, and love are an inspiration to me and a profound influence on my life. May I live true to the heritage they gave me, so that in what I say and do I may reflect their lives and witness to the saving message of Jesus Christ.

M.B.

The Making of a Saint

Holy Spirit, I pray today in union with all the unsung heroes and heroines I have met throughout my life who are now with you in their heavenly home. They were blessed with a faith as strong as a rock and yet as gentle as a soft breeze. They trusted God as their Father no matter what tragedies or difficulties came their way. Their love shone through in a way that gave the word *love* a new meaning and dimension.

This morning as I join my prayers with them in their heavenly home, I give you thanks for bestowing on me the grace and privilege of sharing my life with them.

M.B.

Beacons of Hope

Holy Spirit, we thank you that in every age you were the Counselor and Inspirer of many people who in times of darkness were a light to the world and a beacon of hope to others who felt overpowered by doubt, disbelief, and hostility. We join our prayers today with theirs, so that with them as our inspiration, we may go out to meet our world with confidence and hope and be a light of Christ and a beacon of hope to everyone we meet.

M.B.

For All Who Yearn for Meaning to Life

Holy Spirit, conscious of our blessing as members of your family and the privilege of being known as Christian, we pray in union with the saints for all those who yearn for a purpose and meaning to life and a faith to sustain them. Breathe on them, Breath of God, and give them wisdom, insight, and faith to commit their lives to the gospel of Jesus Christ and be living members of our family, the communion of saints.

M.B.

The Meaning of Greatness

Holy Spirit, you alone are the Inspirer of the saints and holy people who have a true understanding of the meaning of life. Help us in our confused world to retain a firm grip on what constitutes greatness, happiness, and fulfillment. The saints lived lives that would not attract the media, which creates "stars" of glitz, glamour, and wealth. Help us today to look upwards to the saints who are our models of true wholeness rather than earthwards on "stars" who appear for a short time only to disappear from view, leaving no message of the real meaning of life.

M.B.

Mementos of the Saints

Lord Jesus Christ, because you were human, you understand how we need physical reminders of your presence on earth. Because of our desire to be close to you, we venerate the cross and wear it as a sign of our commitment to you. In a lesser way, because you are unique and the only Mediator between your Father and us, we are encouraged in our lives and prayers by the pictures, paintings, sculptures, medals, and such that remind us of our Lady and all the saints. May we never feel the need to apologize for a devotion, which has always been the hallmark of the church. May we use the mementos in such a way that they bring us closer to you and all the saints.

M.B.

Filled With the Spirit

O God our Father,
source of all holiness,
the work of your hands is manifest in your saints,
the beauty of your truth is reflected in their faith.

May we, who aspire to have part in their joy, be filled
with the Spirit that blessed their lives, so that, having
shared their faith on earth, we may also know their peace
in your kingdom.

M.B.

The Fellowship of the Saints

For all the saints, who from their labors rest,
Who thee by faith before the world confessed,
Thy name, O Jesus, be forever blest.
Alleluia, alleluia!

Thou wast their Rock, their Fortress, and their Might;
Thou, Lord, their Captain in the well-fought fight;
Thou in the darkness drear their one true Light.

O may thy soldiers, faithful, true and bold,
Fight as the saints who nobly fought of old,
And win, with them, the victor's crown of gold.

O blest communion! Fellowship divine!
We feebly struggle, they in glory shine;
Yet all are one in thee, for all are thine.

The golden evening brightens in the west;
Soon, soon to faithful warriors cometh rest;
Sweet is the calm of paradise the blest.

But lo! There breaks a yet more glorious day;
The saints triumphant rise in bright array;
The King of glory passes on his way.

From earth's wide bounds, from ocean's farthest coast,
Through gates of pearl streams in the countless host,
Singing to Father, Son, and Holy Ghost,
Alleluia, alleluia!

William How